The **Complete Guide** to the

duolingo
english test

SIWONSCHOOL
LAB

The Complete Guide to the Duolingo English Test (DET)

Copyright © 2023 by SJW International
First published 2022
Printed in the Republic of Korea

Author SIWONSCHOOL Lab, Jenny
ISBN 979-11-6150-740-8 13740

SIWONSCHOOL
www.siwonschool.com

SIWONSCHOOL LAB
lab.siwonschool.com

Introduction

Who is this book for?

This book is designed for test takers of any level aiming to take the Duolingo English Test (DET). Whether you are just starting to prepare or about to take the test, this book can help you achieve your target score for the upcoming DET.

Why should you use this book?

The materials in this book are based on actual Duolingo English Tests administered between March 2021 and July 2023 and provide a comprehensive overview of DET. You can find strategies and study tips as well as a range of exercise questions for all 13 question types. In addition, there is a full practice test at the end of the book that will give you an authentic test-taking experience.

Contents

Chapter 1. DET Question Types

Chapter 2. DET Practice Test

Appendix

How to Use this Book

| All About DET

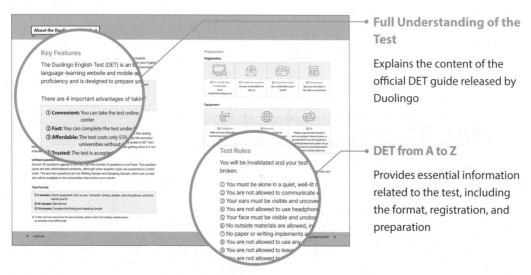

Full Understanding of the Test

Explains the content of the official DET guide released by Duolingo

DET from A to Z

Provides essential information related to the test, including the format, registration, and preparation

| DET Question Types

Detailed Analysis of all 13 Question Types

Introduces and analyzes each question type including its key points, strategies, and study tips

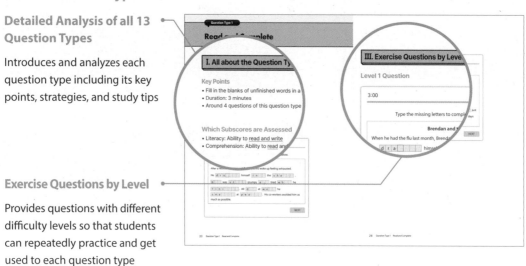

Exercise Questions by Level

Provides questions with different difficulty levels so that students can repeatedly practice and get used to each question type

| DET Practice Test

Practice Test

Presents a full practice test with the same format and difficulty as the actual exam

Practice Test Answers

Provides answers for the practice test

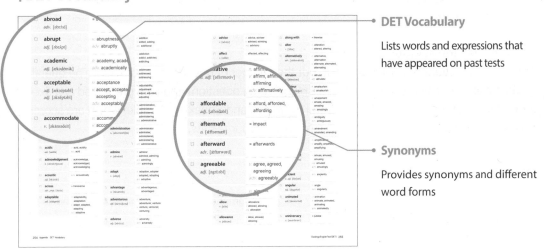

| DET Vocabulary

DET Vocabulary

Lists words and expressions that have appeared on past tests

Synonyms

Provides synonyms and different word forms

About the Duolingo English Test

Key Features

The Duolingo English Test (DET) is an English test made by Duolingo, the most popular language-learning website and mobile application in the world. The test measures your English proficiency and is designed to prepare you for studying in an English-speaking environment.

There are 4 important advantages of taking the test.

> ① **Convenient:** You can take the test online anywhere, anytime without needing to travel to a test center
> ② **Fast:** You can complete the test under ONE hour and receive your results in TWO days
> ③ **Affordable:** The test costs only $59, and you can send your results to an unlimited number of universities without any additional cost
> ④ **Trusted:** The test is accepted by over 4,000 universities around the world

Test System

Computerized adaptive testing

DET is a computer-based test that adapts to the skill level of each test taker. In this testing system, the difficulty of the next question or set of questions is determined by the accuracy of the test taker's answers to the previous questions. There are 3 difficulty levels in DET from level 1 to 3, but it is difficult for test takers to identify which level they are getting since it is not indicated on the test.

Unfixed question numbers

Around 40 questions appear in the test, but the number of questions is not fixed. The question types are also administered randomly, although some question types are presented in a fixed order. The last two questions are the Writing Sample and Speaking Sample, which are scored and will be available to the universities that receive your results.

Test Format

> ① **5 minutes:** Check equipment such as your computer camera, speaker, and microphone, and then submit your ID
> ② **45 minutes:** Take the test
> ③ **10 minutes:** Complete the Writing and Speaking Sample

※ To find out more about how the test proceeds, please check the Duolingo website below:
go.duolingo.com/walkthrough

Preparation

Registration

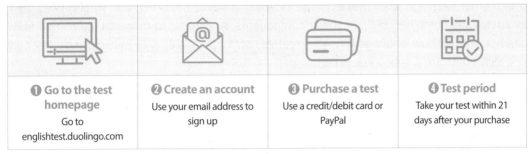

❶ Go to the test homepage	❷ Create an account	❸ Purchase a test	❹ Test period
Go to englishtest.duolingo.com	Use your email address to sign up	Use a credit/debit card or PayPal	Take your test within 21 days after your purchase

Equipment

❶ Computer	❷ Internet	❸ ID
Make sure your computer has a functioning camera, speaker, and microphone	Make sure you have an internet connection of at least 2 Mbps download speed and 1 Mbps upload speed (To check your internet speed, search "internet speed test" and test your speed for free)	Prepare a government-issued ID such as a passport, driver's license, or government ID. Your ID should have your full legal name and a photo of your face. It should be an actual physical ID, not a digital or photocopied one

Test Rules

You will be invalidated and your test results will not be certified if any of the following rules are broken.

① You must be alone in a quiet, well-lit room with all doors closed
② You are not allowed to communicate with another person during the test
③ Your ears must be visible and uncovered
④ You are not allowed to use headphones or earphones
⑤ Your face must be visible and unobscured
⑥ No outside materials are allowed, including mobile devices, writing instruments, or notes
⑦ You are not allowed to take notes during the test
⑧ You are not allowed to use any predictive text programs
⑨ You are not allowed to leave the test window on your app for any reason
⑩ You are not allowed to look away from the screen during the test

Test Scores

Subscores

Unlike other language tests that evaluate listening, reading, speaking, and writing skills, DET evaluates the combined skills of these components. According to research, combined skills can better show how language is used in real life, where people employ multiple skills, not only one skill. There are 4 subscores in DET.

> ① **Literacy:** Your ability to read and write
>
> ② **Comprehension:** Your ability to read and listen
>
> ③ **Conversation:** Your ability to listen and speak
>
> ④ **Production:** Your ability to write and speak

The overall score and subscores are graded on a scale from 10 to 160. Your score certificate is valid for 2 years.

How the questions are scored

> ① **Computer:** Your test is graded through methods developed specifically for each question type
>
> ② **Human proctor:** Trained proctors review your recorded test
>
> ③ **Partial credit:** If you get only a part of the answer correct in one question, you will still be able to receive partial credit

How each question type is scored

Question types with correct answers are graded automatically by comparing the similarities and differences between your responses and the correct answers. Question types with open response questions do not have a "correct" answer and are evaluated according to the following scoring criteria.

① The correctness of your grammar (grammatical accuracy)
② The variety and level of your grammar (grammatical complexity)
③ The level of vocabulary used (lexical sophistication)
④ The variety of word choice (lexical diversity)
⑤ How well you answer the question that was asked (task relevance)
⑥ How much you can say or write in a limited time (fluency)
⑦ The pronunciation and pace of your speech (acoustic features; for speaking questions only)

No.	Question Type	Note
1	Read and Complete	Graded automatically by comparing your responses to the correct answers. (There is no additional deduction for submitting blanks or typing incorrect answers.)
2	Read and Select	Graded automatically by comparing your responses to the correct answers.
3	Listen and Type	Graded automatically by comparing your responses to the correct answers. (A missing word is penalized more than a mistyped word.)
4	Read Aloud	Graded automatically by comparing your responses to the correct answers.
5	Write About the Photo	Graded according to the scoring criteria for open response questions.
6	Speak About the Photo	Graded according to the scoring criteria for open response questions.
7	Read, Then Write	Graded according to the scoring criteria for open response questions.
8	Read, Then Speak	Graded according to the scoring criteria for open response questions.
9	Listen, Then Speak	Graded according to the scoring criteria for open response questions.
10	Interactive Reading	Graded automatically by comparing your responses to the correct answers.
11	Interactive Listening	Graded automatically by comparing your responses to the correct answers. *The Summarize the Conversation question is graded according to the scoring criteria for open response questions.
12	Writing Sample	Graded according to the scoring criteria for open response questions.
13	Speaking Sample	Graded according to the scoring criteria for open response questions.

General Comparison

The table below shows a comparison between DET, TOEFL, and IELTS, which are currently the most popular exams for international students aiming to study abroad.

	DET	TOEFL	IELTS
Subscores	Literacy Comprehension Conversation Production	Reading Listening Speaking Writing	Reading Listening Speaking Writing
Method of Delivery	Computer with internet connection	Computer with internet connection	Either paper or computer
Fee	$59(USD)	$210(USD)	$245~$255(USD)
Duration	Less than 1 hour	Around 2 hours	Around 2 hours and 45 minutes
Overall Score	10-160	0-120	0-9
Delivery of Result	Within 2 days	Between 4 to 8 days	Paper: Within 13 days Computer: Between 3 to 5 days
Vocabulary	Words you encounter in everyday life and vocabulary used in college essays or textbooks	Academic vocabulary and terminology used in university lectures and textbooks	Academic vocabulary and terminology used in university lectures and academic journals

Merits of DET

DET covers the essentials of English differently compared to other English proficiency tests. It contains less academic vocabulary and terminology than TOEFL or IELTS. The questions are short and straightforward, so they are approachable for students with various levels of English proficiency.

Score Comparison

An estimated score conversion between DET, TOEFL, and IELTS is calculated below.

DET	TOEFL iBT	IELTS
160	120	8.5–9.0
155	119	8.0
150	117–118	
145	113–116	7.5
140	109–112	
135	104–108	7.0
130	98–103	
125	93–97	6.5
120	87–92	
115	82–86	
110	76–81	6.0
105	70–75	
100	65–69	5.5
95	59–64	
90	53–58	
85	47–52	5.0
80	41–46	
75	35–40	
70	30–34	4.5
65	24–29	
10–60	0–23	0–4.0

Scores required by most universities

Immerse Yourself in English

Speaking

① Talk to yourself in English whenever you have time alone

② Repeat what you hear while watching movies or videos in English

③ Search online or watch YouTube videos for guides on how to correct your pronunciation when you are having trouble with some English sounds

Writing

① Write your shopping list and to-do list in English

② Install an English keyboard on your phone and practice using English to text, search, and post on social media

③ Join online communities that use English and write comments in English

Reading

① Read blogs and follow social media accounts in English

② Read news articles in English and expand your vocabulary on current events

③ Read your favorite books in English

Listening

① Listen to music in English and check what you hear with the lyrics

② Set the audio and subtitles to English when watching shows or movies

③ Listen to podcasts in English on topics you are interested in

Take the Practice Tests as Many Times as Possible

If you create an account and log in to the Duolingo English Test homepage, you can take the practice tests for free. The practice tests are a 30-minute version of the actual exam with the same format and difficulty. Therefore, candidates preparing for DET are encouraged to take the practice tests as many times as possible to build familiarity and confidence.

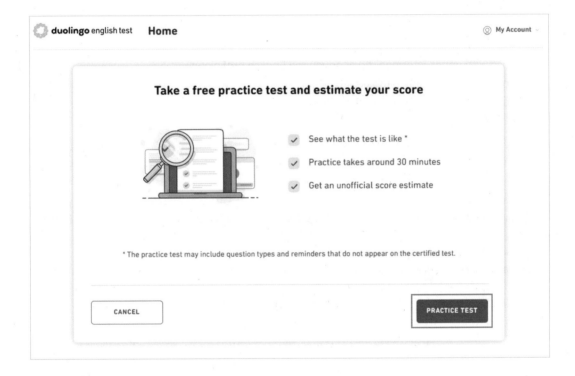

- Study every day by referring to the following study plans according to your English level.

- Solve problems in a testing environment by setting a time limit and making sure you are not interrupted. Always review the questions and your answers afterwards.

- Complete this book several times. Each time you go over the same material, you will find the questions less challenging and improve your time.

One-Week Study Plan

- For those with upper-intermediate or advanced English proficiency
- For those who are already familiar with DET
- For those who want to have a quick review before taking the test

Day 1	Day 2	Day 3	Day 4	Day 5
Question Type 1: Read and Complete **Question Type 2:** Read and Select **Question Type 3:** Listen and Type	**Question Type 4:** Read Aloud **Question Type 5:** Write About the Photo **Question Type 6:** Speak About the Photo	**Question Type 7:** Read, Then Write **Question Type 8:** Read, Then Speak **Question Type 9:** Listen, Then Speak	**Question Type 10:** Interactive Reading	**Question Type 11:** Interactive Listening

Day 6	Day 7
Question Type 12: Writing Sample **Question Type 13:** Speaking Sample	**Practice Test**

20-Day Study Plan

- For those with beginner or intermediate English proficiency
- For those taking the test for the first time

Day 1	Day 2	Day 3	Day 4	Day 5
About the Duolingo English Test DET vs TOEFL vs IELTS How to Prepare for DET	**Question Type 1:** Read and Complete	**Question Type 2:** Read and Select	**Question Type 3:** Listen and Type	**Question Type 4:** Read Aloud
Day 6	**Day 17**	**Day 8**	**Day 9**	**Day 10**
Question Type 5: Write About the Photo	**Question Type 6:** Speak About the Photo	**Question Type 7:** Read, Then Write	**Question Type 8:** Read, Then Speak	**Question Type 9:** Listen, Then Speak
Day 11	**Day 12**	**Day 13**	**Day 14**	**Day 15**
Review Question Types 1-9	**Question Type 10:** Interactive Reading	**Question Type 11:** Interactive Listening	**Question Type 12:** Writing Sample	**Question Type 13:** Speaking Sample
Day 16	**Day 17**	**Day 18**	**Day 19**	**Day 20**
Review Question Types 10-13	**Practice Test**	Review Practice Test	**Appendix:** DET Vocabulary	**Appendix:** DET Vocabulary

Chapter

1

DET Question Types

Read and Complete

I. All about the Question Type

Key Points

- Fill in the blanks of unfinished words in a passage
- Duration: 3 minutes
- Around 4 questions of this question type appear in random order

Which Subscores are Assessed

- Literacy: Ability to <u>read and write</u>
- Comprehension: Ability to <u>read</u> and listen

How the Question is Presented

① The question will appear on the screen when the timer begins.

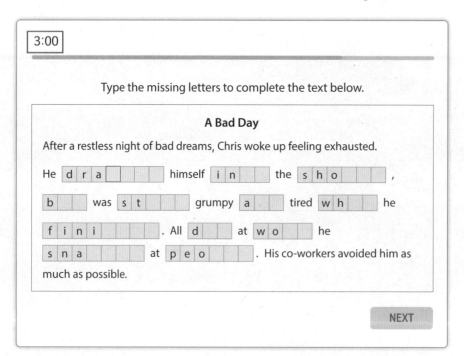

② Read the whole passage. Type the missing letters, using the given letters as hints.

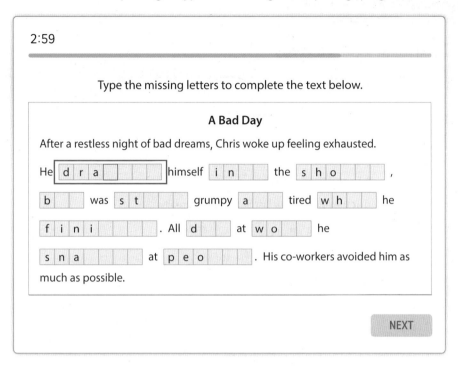

③ If you finish typing before the time limit, proofread your answers. Click NEXT to go to the next question. The next question will automatically appear when the time expires.

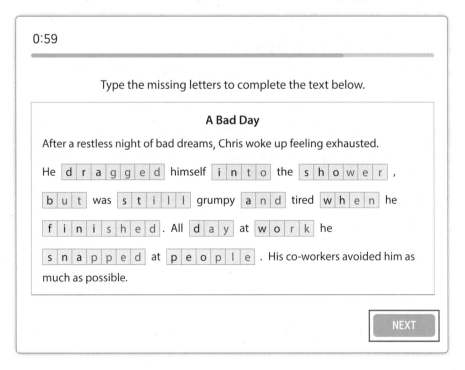

II. Strategies and Study Tips

Strategy 1. Determine Your Strategy

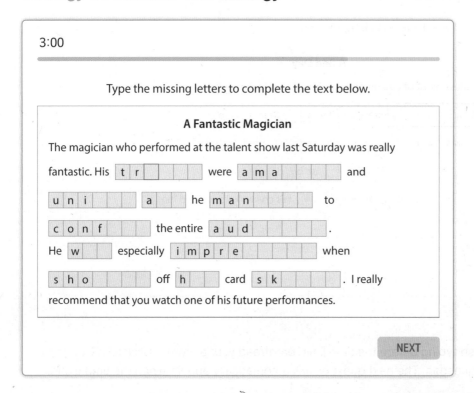

3:00

Type the missing letters to complete the text below.

A Fantastic Magician

The magician who performed at the talent show last Saturday was really fantastic. His t r ☐ ☐ ☐ were a m a ☐ ☐ ☐ and u n i ☐ ☐ a ☐ he m a n ☐ ☐ to c o n f ☐ ☐ the entire a u d ☐ ☐ ☐ ☐ . He w ☐ ☐ especially i m p r e ☐ ☐ ☐ ☐ when s h o ☐ ☐ ☐ off h ☐ ☐ card s k ☐ ☐ ☐ ☐ . I really recommend that you watch one of his future performances.

NEXT

STEP 1 **Understand the context of the passage**

Read the first and last sentences first, as they will help you understand the context of the passage.

The magician who performed at the talent show last Saturday was really fantastic.

I really recommend that you watch one of his future performances.

★ Your understanding: The magician's performance was fantastic (context clues: magician, performance, fantastic)

STEP 2 **Complete the words using context clues and word classes**

Use context clues to deduce related words. In addition, you also need to consider the word classes, such as noun, verb, adjective, adverb, preposition, conjunction, etc., that would be appropriate for the sentence structure and word form.

Context Clues	Related Words
magician	tricks, audience, card skills
performance, fantastic	amazing, unique, impressive, show off

The magician who performed at the talent show last Saturday was really fantastic. His tricks
                                                                                                noun(plural)

were amazing and unique, and he managed to confuse the entire audience. He was especially
      adjective   adjective conjunction   verb(past) manage to + infinitive   noun   be verb (past)

impressive when showing off his card skills. I really recommend that you watch one of his future
adjective   participle phrase possessive noun(plural)

performances.

STEP 3 **Finalize and proofread your answer**

If there are blanks skipped in the middle, complete them using other filled-in words. If there is time left, check whether the entire text flows naturally.

The magician who performed at the talent show last Saturday was really fantastic. His tricks were amazing and unique, and he managed to confuse the entire audience. He was especially impressive when showing off his card skills. I really recommend that you watch one of his future performances.

Tip

Here are some common topics that frequently appear in Question Type 1 passages.

1. Informative: Excerpts from academic topics such as geography, science, and art
2. Literature: Excerpts from various titles (like the Harry Potter series)
3. Narrative: Everyday events
4. Dialogue: Everyday conversation
5. Instructive: Explanation of processes

Strategy 2. **Memorize Common Words**

Short Words that Appear Frequently

Be Verbs	be / am, are, is / was, were
Prepositions (Place & Time)	at, on, in / from, to / for, during / by, near across, around, out, throughout (also adverbs)
Prepositions (Cause & Object)	for, of, to, with, about, on
Modals	can, may, will
Pronouns	you, we, he, she, they, it (subject) my, your, our, his, her, their, its (possessive) me, you, us, him, her, them, it (object)
Demonstrative Pronouns	this, that, these, those
Indefinite Pronouns	all, one, anything some, any, many, much (also adjectives)
Articles	a, an, the
Conjunctions	and, but, or, because, when, while as, than, before, after (also prepositions)
Adjectives	every, other each (also a pronoun) such, next (also adverbs)
Adverbs	almost, also, again, always, even, still, far, soon, too / not, never / here, there

Questions

1 There [a   ] paintings [o   ] presidents [f r   ] different countries.

2 This feature [i] usually found [i] movies.

3 She was passionate [a   ] [h   ] job, [b   ] she was recently fired from her work.

Answers

1 are, of, from

2 is, in

3 about, her, but

Strategy 3. Study for Your Target Score

For DET 100+ Scores

- **Deal with the short blanks first.**

- There are quite a few short blank questions, so practice in order to not make mistakes on them.
- Memorize the "Short Words that Appear Frequently" in this book. Do not forget to look at the sentence structure.

- **Pay attention to -s/ed/er/est**

- -s/-es or -d/-ed can be added after a verb or noun depending on the number of objects or the tense.
- Similarly, the comparative or superlative ending of -er/-est can be added after an adjective or adverb.

- **Be sure to memorize words you do not know**

- DET repeatedly comes up with similar topics, so make sure to memorize the words you do not know while studying this book.
- Memorize both the spelling and definition of vocabulary words to fill in the blanks correctly.

For DET 120+ Scores

- **Memorize vocabulary about various topics**

- Get familiar with common topics and vocabulary that appear in Read and Complete questions by answering various questions.
- Memorize related words for each topic so that you can deduce the words to fill in the blanks according to the topic.

- **Memorize synonyms together**

- Since the synonyms of words in the first and last sentence are frequently asked in blanks, memorize the synonyms and their spelling together with vocabulary words.
- Refer to the Appendix for synonyms and different word forms of vocabulary words.

- **Understanding the context**

- For high-level (level 3) questions, learn to deduce words by understanding the context of the passage.
- Practice understanding the context by combining the words between the blanks as well as the first and last sentences.

III. Exercise Questions by Level

Level 1 Question

3:00

Type the missing letters to complete the text below.

Brendan and the Flu

When he had the flu last month, Brendan felt like he could barely move.

He `d r a` ⬜⬜⬜ himself `i n` ⬜ the `s h o` ⬜⬜ ,

`b` ⬜ he `s t` ⬜⬜⬜ felt achy `a` ⬜ `t i` ⬜⬜⬜

`w h` ⬜ he got `o` ⬜⬜ . He `t` ⬜⬜⬜ his boss `t h` ⬜⬜

he `n e` ⬜⬜⬜⬜ to take a couple `o` ⬜ days `o` ⬜⬜ , `a` ⬜⬜ just

`s t a` ⬜⬜⬜ at `h o` ⬜⬜ and `r e s` ⬜⬜⬜ . After a few days

of rest and flu medication, he finally began to feel better.

NEXT

STEP 1 **Understand the context of the passage**

Read the first and last sentences first, as they will help you understand the context of the passage.

When he had the flu last month, Brendan felt like he could barely move.

After a few days of rest and flu medication, he finally began to feel better.

★ Your understanding: Brendan had the flu and barely moved (context clues: flu, barely moved)

STEP 2 **Complete the words using context clues and word classes**

Use context clues to deduce related words. In addition, you also need to consider the word classes, such as noun, verb, adjective, adverb, preposition, conjunction, etc., that would be appropriate for the sentence structure and word form.

Context Clues	Related Words
flu	tired, stay home, rest
barely moved	drag oneself

When he had the flu last month, Brendan felt like he could barely move. He dragged himself into the shower, but he still felt achy and tired when he got out. He told his boss that he needed to take a couple of days off, and just stayed at home and rested. After a few days of rest and flu medication, he finally began to feel better.

★ Note the past tense of the passage → Use the past tense of the verb!

STEP 3 **Finalize and proofread your answer**

If there are blanks skipped in the middle, complete them using other filled-in words. If there is time left, check whether the entire text flows naturally.

When he had the flu last month, Brendan felt like he could barely move. He dragged himself into the shower, but he still felt achy and tired when he got out. He told his boss that he needed to take a couple of days off, and just stayed at home and rested. After a few days of rest and flu medication, he finally began to feel better.

Level 2 Question

3:00

Type the missing letters to complete the text below.

Symptoms of Alzheimer's Disease

The early symptoms of Alzheimer's disease vary from one person to the next.

O___ of t___ first s i _____ o__ cognitive

i m p_____ related to Alzheimer's i__ memory

l o___ . Sufferers a_____ commonly h_____ difficulty

c h o_____ the correct words to s____ , forget why

t h____ have entered a room, and make poor decisions due to impaired

reasoning and judgement. As the disease progresses, memory loss and

cognitive difficulties typically worsen.

NEXT

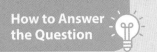
STEP 1 **Understand the context of the passage**

Read the first and last sentences first, as they will help you understand the context of the passage.

The early symptoms of Alzheimer's disease vary from one person to the next.

As the disease progresses, these memory loss and cognitive difficulties typically worsen.

★ Your understanding: The symptoms of Alzheimer's disease vary (context clues: symptoms, disease)

STEP 2 **Complete the words using context clues and word classes**

Use context clues to deduce related words. In addition, you also need to consider the word classes, such as noun, verb, adjective, adverb, preposition, conjunction, etc., that would be appropriate for the sentence structure and word form.

Context Clues	Related Words
symptoms	signs, difficulties
disease	impairment, loss, suffer

> The early symptoms of Alzheimer's disease vary from one person to the next. One of the first signs of cognitive impairment related to Alzheimer's is memory loss. Sufferers also commonly have difficulty choosing the correct words to say, forget why they have entered a room, and make poor decisions due to impaired reasoning and judgement. As the disease progresses, memory loss and cognitive difficulties typically worsen.

STEP 3 **Finalize and proofread your answer**

If there are blanks skipped in the middle, complete them using other filled-in words. If there is time left, check whether the entire text flows naturally.

The early symptoms of Alzheimer's disease vary from one person to the next. One of the first signs of cognitive impairment related to Alzheimer's is memory loss. Sufferers also commonly have difficulty choosing the correct words to say, forget why they have entered a room, and make poor decisions due to impaired reasoning and judgement. As the disease progresses, memory loss and cognitive difficulties typically worsen.

3:00

Type the missing letters to complete the text below.

The Smallest Country in the World

Vatican City is the smallest country in the world, although it is sometimes referred to as a city-state. The `c` `i` `‎` `i` `‎` completely `s` `u` `r` `r` `‎` `‎` `‎` `‎` `‎` by Rome `a` `‎` `‎` occupies `a` `‎` `a` `‎` `‎` `‎` of `r` `o` `u` `‎` `‎` `‎` 110 acres. Due to `i` `‎` `‎` small size, `t` `‎` `‎` city cannot `a` `c` `c` `o` `‎` `‎` `‎` `‎` `‎` all `o` `‎` `‎` its `b` `u` `i` `‎` `‎` `‎` `‎` `‎` . Therefore, a special privilege is `e` `x` `‎` `‎` `‎` `‎` `‎` to some of its `s` `t` `r` `u` `‎` `‎` `‎` `‎` `w` `h` `‎` `‎` `‎` are `s` `i` `t` `‎` `‎` `‎` `‎` `‎` in Rome, and this includes the pope's summer `r` `e` `s` `i` `‎` `‎` `‎` `‎` . The Vatican is ranked as the smallest state in the world right behind Monaco and Nauru.

NEXT

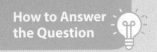
STEP 1 **Understand the whole context of the passage**

Read the first and last sentences first, as they will help you understand the context of the passage.

Vatican City is the smallest country in the world, although it is sometimes referred to as a city-state.

The Vatican is ranked as the smallest state in the world right behind Monaco and Nauru.

★ Your understanding: Vatican City, the smallest country in the world (context clues: city, smallest country)

STEP 2 **Complete the words using context clues and word classes**

Use context clues to deduce related words. In addition, you also need to consider the word classes, such as noun, verb, adjective, adverb, preposition, conjunction, etc., that would be appropriate for the sentence structure and word form.

Context Clues	Related Words
city	area, structures, situated, residence
smallest country	size, accommodate

Vatican City is the smallest country in the world, although it is sometimes referred to as a city-state. The city is completely surrounded by Rome and occupies an area of roughly 110 acres. Due to its small size, the city cannot accommodate all of its buildings. Therefore, a special privilege is extended to some of its structures which are situated in Rome, and this includes the pope's summer residence. The Vatican is ranked as the smallest state in the world right behind Monaco and Nauru.

★ Note that most verbs in the passage are in the passive voice.

STEP 3 **Finalize and proofread your answer**

If there are blanks skipped in the middle, complete them using other filled-in words. If there is time left, check whether the entire text flows naturally.

Vatican City is the smallest country in the world, although it is sometimes referred to as a city-state. The city is completely surrounded by Rome and occupies an area of roughly 110 acres. Due to its small size, the city cannot accommodate all of its buildings. Therefore, a special privilege is extended to some of its structures which are situated in Rome, and this includes the pope's summer residence. The Vatican is ranked as the smallest state in the world right behind Monaco and Nauru.

Read and Select

I. All about the Question Type

Key Points

- Select the real English words on the screen
- Duration: 1 minute
- Around 4 questions of this question type appear in random order

Which Subscores are Assessed

- Literacy: Ability to read and write
- Comprehension: Ability to read and listen

How the Question is Presented

① The question will appear on the screen when the timer begins.

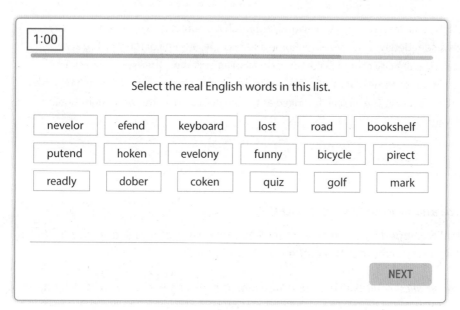

② Choose the real English words by focusing on the spelling of each word.

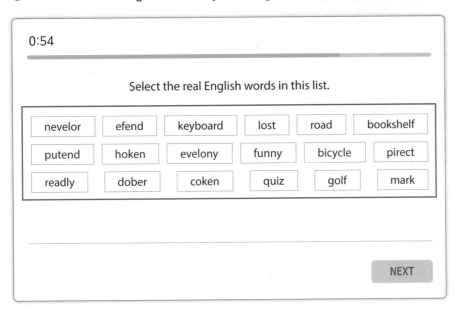

③ When you have finished selecting the words, click NEXT to go to the next question.

II. Strategies and Study Tips

Strategy 1. Determine Your Strategy

```
1:00
──────────────────────────────────────────

              Select the real English words in this list.

  deliberation    unstood    affordant    septional    monitor    grimace

  instill     thread     cronered     ability     splending     bearity

  grince     bevery     fluctuate     ospouse     legible     marose


                                                        NEXT
```

STEP 1 **Carefully read each word**

Focus on the spelling of each word.

deliberation	unstood	affordant	septional	monitor	grimace
instill	thread	cronered	ability	splending	bearity
grince	bevery	fluctuate	ospouse	legible	marose

STEP 2 **Eliminate fake words**

Fake words are similar to real words, so be careful when you distinguish the real words from the list.

Fake Word	Real Word	Fake Word	Real Word
unstood	stood	bearity	beauty / bearing
affordant	affordable	grince	prince
septional	sectional / exceptional	bevery	beverage
cronered	cornered	ospouse	spouse
splending	splendid / spending	marose	morose / arose

Select the real words

Select the real words. If a word seems confusing, exclude it as confusing words are usually fake.

deliberation	unstood	affordant	septional	monitor	grimace
instill	thread	cronered	ability	splending	bearity
grince	bevery	fluctuate	ospouse	legible	marose

Strategy 2. **Memorize Common Prefixes and Suffixes**

Prefixes to memorize

A prefix is a letter or group of letters added at the beginning of a word to make a new word. Many fake words in the test are combined with incorrect prefixes. To avoid selecting fake words, memorize the following prefixes along with examples of words that contain each prefix.

Prefix	DET Vocabulary	Prefix	DET Vocabulary
co- together, with	coherent coincide colleague collection cooperate coordinate corporation	**dis-** opposite	disability disagree disarray discharge discomfort disillusioned dismount disorder disputable dispute
com- together, with	combination common communication community companion compassion compose composition	**em-/en-** [verb] cause to be something	embarrass embrace empower enable encouraging enhance enlarge enlighten

Prefix	DET Vocabulary	Prefix	DET Vocabulary
ex- former, not including	exchange exclusively exhale exit explore exposure expressed extinction extract extrovert	**mis-** wrong, bad	mishap misinformation misinterpret misjudge mislead misrepresentation mistakenly mistrust misunderstanding misuse
il-/ir- not, opposite	illegal illogical illusion irrational irregular irrelevant irresponsible irreversible	**non-** not, opposite	nondescript nonetheless nonexistent nonfiction nonsense nonspecific nonviolent
im-/in- not, lacking, opposite	impatient impractical improper inaction induce influence injustice insinuate invisible	**over-** above, extremely	overcharge overcome overestimate overflow overlap overlook overly overreact overweight
inter- between, among	interact interchange interference interlude intermediate international interpersonal interrogation interstate	**pre-** before	precaution precedent precondition prediction prelude premature preparation previously

Prefix	DET Vocabulary	Prefix	DET Vocabulary
re- again	recall reconstruct reminiscent renewable reset retrieve revert review revise revival	**trans-** across, beyond, change	transatlantic transfer transform transit transition transitive translation transport
semi- half, not completely	semiannual semicircle semicolon semiconductor semiconscious semiformal	**un-** not, lacking, opposite	uncompromising undemanding undeniable undo unlikely unplug unproductive unscrupulous unstable unwise
sub- under, below, nearly	subjunction submarine submerge submissive subordinate subsequently substandard suburban	**under-** below, less than	undercut underestimate underground underlie undermine understated undertake undertaker underwear

A suffix is a letter or group of letters added at the end of a word to make a new word. Like prefixes, suffixes are often used to make fake words in the test.

Suffix	DET Vocabulary	Suffix	DET Vocabulary
-able/-ible *adj.* able to do	adjustable capable comfortable inevitable profitable reasonable reliable replaceable suitable valuable	**-en** *v.* to become or cause to be *adj.* made of, consisting of	brighten fasten frighten golden lessen sharpen sunken weaken wooden
-ant/-ent *n.* person or thing doing a specified thing *adj.* doing a specified thing	assistant attendant consultant descendant fragrant observant reluctant significant vacant	**-er/-or** *n.* person or thing associated with something	admirer cleaner contender customer manufacturer supervisor supporter thermometer visitor
-ary *n.* thing or person connected with *adj.* relating to, connected with	dictionary elementary honorary military missionary monetary planetary secretary sedentary voluntary	**-ful** *adj.* full of, having the qualities of	bountiful colorful doubtful frightful helpful. merciful resourceful rightful truthful useful
-ed *v.* past simple and past participle of a verb *adj.* having, characterized by	alleged cliched extended insulted interested motivated reduced related sacred terrified	**-ing** *n.* gerund(made from a verb and used like a noun) *v.* present participle of a verb *adj.* continuous action	amazing depressing disputing encouraging fascinating humiliating intoxicating promising rewarding underlying

Suffix	DET Vocabulary	Suffix	DET Vocabulary
-ion/-sion/-tion *n.* act, process, state, condition, result	allocation attraction confusion evolution extinction isolation subtraction supervision suspension vision	**-ize** *v.* cause to become	emphasize familiarize industrialize maximize minimize personalize rationalize standardize
-ism *n.* act, practice, or process of doing something	altruism communism criticism idealism materialism mechanism optimism realism utilitarianism	**-less** *adj.* without something	aimless ceaseless faultless fearless helpless merciless restless thoughtless valueless
-ity *n.* quality, state, degree	capability credibility diversity mediocrity mortality priority proximity scarcity validity vicinity	**-ly** *adv.* in a specified manner or way	abruptly capriciously consistently incredibly moderately obstinately preferably readily sufficiently unnecessarily
-ive/-ous *adj.* doing or tending to do something specified	adventurous ambiguous capricious cautious corrosive excessive notorious outrageous predictive voracious	**-ment** *n.* action, process, result, state, condition	achievement acknowledgement amusement contentment enrollment involvement movement requirement tournament treatment

Suffix	DET Vocabulary	Suffix	DET Vocabulary
-ness *n.* state, condition, quality	attractiveness brightness fitness forgiveness kindness preciseness stubbornness toughness wickedness willingness	**-th** *n.* action, process	aftermath childbirth dearth death depth growth length truth warmth wealth
-ship *n.* state, condition, position, status	championship citizenship friendship hardship ownership partnership relationship		

Strategy 3. **Study for Your Target Score**

For DET 100+ Scores

• **Focus on the spelling of each word**

  - The test does not ask for the meaning of the word, so focus on learning the spelling of words.
  - Be careful with familiar words. Only one letter may have been changed, making them incorrect.

• **Know when to exclude words**

  - Choose the words you know with confidence.
  - Exclude the words that you are unsure of. They are most likely fake words that have been changed to be similar to real words.

For DET 120+ Scores

• **Check the prefixes and suffixes**

  - Be aware of incorrect answers that combine a word with the wrong prefix or suffix.
  - Memorize words with a prefix or suffix as one chunk. It can be more confusing if you memorize them while thinking about the meaning of the prefix or suffix.

• **Do not choose a word you have never seen before**

  - Remember that the difficulty of words gradually increases because of the adaptive testing method.
  - If there is a word that you have never seen before, it is most likely a fake word.

III. Exercise Questions by Level

Level 1 Question [1]

1:00

Select the real English words in this list.

pastional	edition	accountant	manderer	enhanced	collatering
viable	scrane	clount	blace	currency	invariably
provered	importanting	confined	mythical	confusion	antelope

NEXT

How to Answer the Question

STEP 1 Carefully read each word

Focus on the spelling of each word.

STEP 2 Eliminate fake words

Fake Word	Real Word	Fake Word	Real Word
pastional	passion	clount	clown
manderer	murderer	blace	brace
collatering	collecting	provered	proved
scrane	crane	importanting	important

STEP 3 Select the real words

pastional	edition	accountant	manderer	enhanced	collatering
viable	scrane	clount	blace	currency	invariably
provered	importanting	confined	mythical	confusion	antelope

Level 1 Question [2]

1:00

Select the real English words in this list.

incentive	travels	milch	chevery	announcer	vilify
industrious	branshy	countly	sinicator	condever	astrologist
rasputed	fault	generable	artery	melpony	overtast

NEXT

How to Answer the Question

STEP 1 Carefully read each word

Focus on the spelling of each word.

STEP 2 Eliminate fake words

Fake Word	Real Word	Fake Word	Real Word
milch	milk	condever	condemn
chevery	cherry	rasputed	disputed
branshy	branch	generable	general
countly	country county	melpony	melody
sinicator	sinister indicator	overtast	overcast

STEP 3 Select the real words

incentive	travels	milch	chevery	announcer	vilify
industrious	branshy	countly	sinicator	condever	astrologist
rasputed	fault	generable	artery	melpony	overtast

Level 2 Question [1]

1:00

Select the real English words in this list.

primate	cramel	disunder	pendulum	assotive	yell
exprane	misvert	polarizing	watancy	histrobic	tendency
maxinly	denuber	biofern	aminted	consolidate

NEXT

How to Answer the Question

STEP 1 Carefully read each word

Focus on the spelling of each word.

STEP 2 Eliminate fake words

Fake Word	Real Word
cramel	camel
disunder	disorder
assotive	assertive assorted
exprane	explain
misvert	divert invert

Fake Word	Real Word
watancy	warranty
histrobic	historic
maxinly	mainly
denuber	denude
biofern	biofuel
aminted	animated

STEP 3 Select the real words

primate	cramel	disunder	pendulum	assotive	yell
exprane	misvert	polarizing	watancy	histrobic	tendency
maxinly	denuber	biofern	aminted	consolidate	

Level 2 Question [2]

1:00

Select the real English words in this list.

stunned	pervasted	torficient	somalter	inbumble	obligiant
vonity	franchise	calority	invasive	subjugate	mutually
expanger	lubricant	facetious	beneful	voracious	emfast

NEXT

How to Answer the Question

STEP 1 Carefully read each word
Focus on the spelling of each word.

STEP 2 Eliminate fake words

Fake Word	Real Word		Fake Word	Real Word
pervasted	devastated		vonity	vanity
torficient	proficient sufficient		calority	calorie calamity
somalter	smelter		expanger	expunge
inbumble	bumble		beneful	benefit
obligiant	obligation		emfast	fast

STEP 3 Select the real words

stunned	pervasted	torficient	somalter	inbumble	obligiant
vonity	franchise	calority	invasive	subjugate	mutually
expanger	lubricant	facetious	beneful	voracious	emfast

Level 3 Question [1]

1:00

Select the real English words in this list.

gullibility	vivid	larner	smirt	pollwing	immoral
merstack	disrester	contridey	inherit	cartably	hopeless
attach	esking	brainably	wentedly	unreliable	tenacity

NEXT

How to Answer the Question

STEP 1 Carefully read each word

Focus on the spelling of each word.

STEP 2 Eliminate fake words

Fake Word	Real Word	Fake Word	Real Word
larner	learner	contridey	contribute
smirt	skirt / smirk	cartably	cart
		esking	asking
pollwing	polling	brainably	brain
merstack	haystack	wentedly	went / wanted
disrester	disaster		

STEP 3 Select the real words

gullibility	vivid	larner	smirt	pollwing	immoral
merstack	disrester	contridey	inherit	cartably	hopeless
attach	esking	brainably	wentedly	unreliable	tenacity

Level 3 Question [2]

1:00

Select the real English words in this list.

gustedly	conbobble	outrageous	enforce	luminous	navigation
void	reciprocal	tannity	nunicator	vibrant	irritated
walifes	anderful	dubious	protrude	likeness	bashful

NEXT

How to Answer the Question

STEP 1 Carefully read each word

Focus on the spelling of each word.

STEP 2 Eliminate fake words

Fake Word	Real Word	Fake Word	Real Word
gustedly	disgustedly	nunicator	indicator
conbobble	bobble	walifes	wallet
tannity	tan	anderful	wonderful

STEP 3 Select the real words

gustedly	conbobble	outrageous	enforce	luminous	navigation
void	reciprocal	tannity	nunicator	vibrant	irritated
walifes	anderful	dubious	protrude	likeness	bashful

Listen and Type

I. All About the Question Type

Key Points

- Listen to a person speaking and type what you hear
- You can replay the statement up to two times (three plays total)
- Duration: 1 minute
- Around 6 questions of this question type appear in random order

Which Subscores are Assessed

- Comprehension: Ability to read and <u>listen</u>
- Conversation: Ability to <u>listen</u> and speak

How the Question is Presented

① The question will appear on the screen when the timer begins.

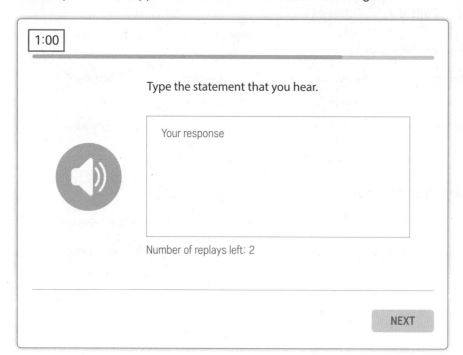

② Type the words you hear first, then replay the statement and fill in the words you missed.

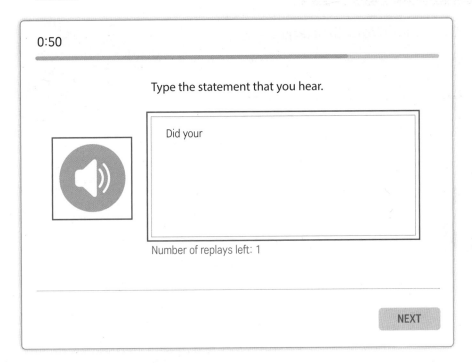

③ If you finish typing before the time limit, proofread your answer. Click NEXT to go to the next question. The next question will automatically appear when the time expires.

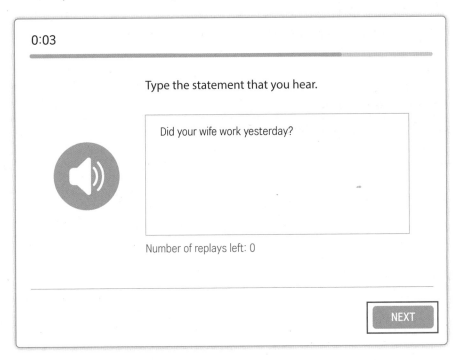

II. Strategies and Study Tips

Strategy 1. Determine Your Strategy

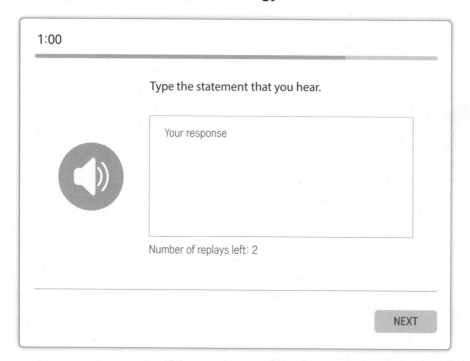

🔊 03-01

STEP 1 **Type out what you hear first**

During the first play, type as many words as you can.

My brother came ... moment ...

STEP 2 **Fill in the words you missed**

For your first replay, fill in the missing words.

My brother came back ... moment ago

STEP 3 **Finalize and double-check your answer**

During your second replay, fill in the articles and prepositions and double-check your answer.

My brother came back a moment ago.

Strategy 2. **Understand Sentence Stress**

Sentence stress

Many English learners, even those who have been studying for several years, still find it hard to understand the speech of native speakers. That is why many learners depend on subtitles when watching movies or shows in English. To improve your English listening skills, you have to understand sentence stress. The rule of sentence stress is simple: content words are stressed while function words are unstressed.

• Content words

A sentence consists of content words and function words. Content words convey the message of the sentence. Generally, content words are nouns, verbs, adjectives, adverbs, names, numbers, etc. They are normally pronounced with greater stress and clarity.

(Example)

Akuma's cast was unveiled in Milan in 1999.
   name   *noun*   *verb*   *name*   *number*

The topic is about students being forced to take science and math classes as part of their major.
   noun   *noun*   *verb*   *verb* *noun*   *noun*   *noun*

• Function words

Unlike content words, function words are grammatical words such as prepositions, articles, pronouns, conjunctions, auxiliary verbs, etc. Function words are weakened by changing their vowel sound to schwa /ə/, giving more prominence to content words.

(Example)

He got an F in history.
      /ən/ /ən/
    article preposition

I told you to listen to her.
      /tə/   /tə/
    article   article

Of course, depending on the context or intention of the speaker, function words can be stressed for the purpose of emphasis and contrast.

(Example)

I do love him!
→ The auxiliary verb "do" is stressed in order to emphasize the speaker's current status of loving him.

The one who broke the car is not him but her.
→ Pronouns are usually unstressed, but the pronouns in this sentence are stressed to convey the key point of the message.

Guessing the missing words

You can still understand the meaning of the sentence through content words, which contain the key message of a sentence.

For example, here is a full sentence that may appear in a question.

I took difficult classes, and I learned a lot from them.

Even if you were not able to catch the full sentence, you can still hear some of the content words, which are often emphasized.

... took ... difficult classes ... learned ... lot ...

You can understand the meaning of the sentence through the content words, and eventually, you can fill in the missing words in relation to the message.

I took difficult classes, and I learned a lot from them.

Tip

These function words frequently appear in DET.

Articles / Conjunctions	Prepositions	Auxiliary verbs
a [ə]	to [tə]	do [də]
an [ən, n]	for [fə(r)]	are [ə(r)]
the [ðə]	from [frəm]	was [wəz]
and [ənd, ən, n̩]	of [ə(v)]	can [kən]
but [bət]	at [əd]	must [məs(t)]

Strategy 3. Study for Your Target Score

For DET 100+ Scores

• **Keep speaking**

- If you cannot speak with the correct pronunciation, you will not be able to hear it correctly, so focus on correcting your pronunciation.
- Frequently practice speaking and learn the pronunciation patterns of English words.

• **Practice with the time limit**

- Set a timer for 1 minute when solving questions.
- Practice typing in English until you can type fast with no typos.

• **Beware of your spelling**

- Typing the correct words but with the wrong spelling affects your score.
- Check your spelling until you run out of time.

For DET 120+ Scores

• **Familiarize yourself with various sentence structures**

- Familiarize yourself with various sentence structures in the DET sample questions. If you understand the sentence structure, you will be able to hear and remember the sentence more easily.
- Build basic English grammar skills. If you understand various sentence structures, you will be able to sort the order of words for confusing questions.

• **Increase your memory span**

- Avoid listening to one or two words at a time. Instead, try to listen to the whole sentence.
- Get into the habit of remembering and writing down several words at once to prepare for long sentences.

• **Do not try to type the whole sentence from the beginning**

- You have 1 minute, so do not try to write the sentence perfectly from your first play.
- Write as many words as possible in abbreviated form and correct the spelling later.

III. Exercise Questions by Level

Level 1 Question [1]

🔊 03-02

How to Answer the Question

STEP 1 **Type the words you hear first**

During the first play, type as many words as you can.

What … preference?

STEP 2 **Fill in the words you missed**

For your first replay, fill in the missing words.

What … your preference?

STEP 3 **Finalize and double-check your answer**

During your second replay, fill in the articles and prepositions and double-check your answer.

What is your preference?

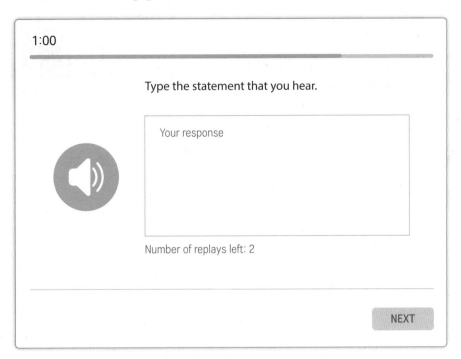

03-03

How to Answer the Question

STEP 1 Type the words you hear first

During the first play, type as many words as you can.

That ... generous ...

STEP 2 Fill in the words you missed

For your first replay, fill in the missing words.

That ... generous ... you

STEP 3 Finalize and double-check your answer

During your second replay, fill in the articles and prepositions and double-check your answer.

That was generous of you.

Level 2 Question [1]

1:00

Type the statement that you hear.

Your response

Number of replays left: 2

NEXT

🔊 03-04

How to Answer the Question

STEP 1 **Type out what you hear first**

During the first play, type as many words as you can.

I appreciate … opportunity … career … firm

STEP 2 **Fill in the words you missed**

For your first replay, fill in the missing words.

I appreciate … opportunity … pursue … career … your firm

STEP 3 **Finalize and double-check your answer**

During your second replay, fill in the articles and prepositions and double-check your answer.

I appreciate the opportunity to pursue a career within your firm.

Level 2 Question [2]

1:00

Type the statement that you hear.

Your response

Number of replays left: 2

NEXT

🔊 03-05

How to Answer the Question

STEP 1 **Type out what you hear first**

During the first play, type as many words as you can.

I aim ... focus ... negative impact ... teenagers ... adults

STEP 2 **Fill in the words you missed**

For your first replay, fill in the missing words.

I aim ... focus ... negative impact ... social media ... teenagers ... young adults

STEP 3 **Finalize and double-check your answer**

During your second replay, fill in the articles and prepositions and double-check your answer.

I aim to focus on the negative impact of social media on teenagers and young adults.

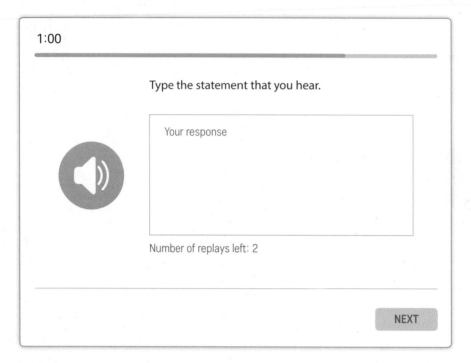

(◁)) 03-06

1:00

Type the statement that you hear.

Your response

Number of replays left: 2

NEXT

How to Answer the Question

STEP 1 **Type out what you hear first**

During the first play, type as many words as you can.

Pilots ... trained ... respond ... potential problems

STEP 2 **Fill in the words you missed**

For your first replay, fill in the missing words.

Pilots ... trained ... respond swiftly ... numerous potential problems

STEP 3 **Finalize and double-check your answer**

During your second replay, fill in the articles and prepositions and double-check your answer.

Pilots are trained to respond swiftly to numerous potential problems.

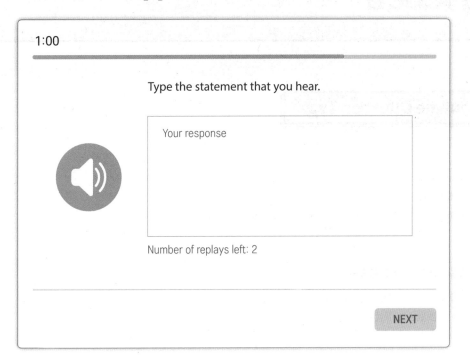

03-07

How to Answer the Question

STEP 1 **Type out what you hear first**

During the first play, type as many words as you can.

Early inhabitants ... created paint ... wide variety ... resources

STEP 2 **Fill in the words you missed**

For your first replay, fill in the missing words.

Early inhabitants ... area created paint pigments ... wide variety ... natural resources

STEP 3 **Finalize and double-check your answer**

During your second replay, fill in the articles and prepositions and double-check your answer.

The early inhabitants of the area created paint pigments from a wide variety of natural resources.

Read Aloud

I. All about the Question Type

Key Points

- Read a written statement and then read it aloud into the microphone
- Duration: 20 seconds
- Around 6 questions of this question type appear in random order

Which Subscores are Assessed

- Comprehension: Ability to <u>read</u> and listen
- Conversation: Ability to listen and <u>speak</u>

How the Question is Presented

① The question will appear on the screen when the timer begins.

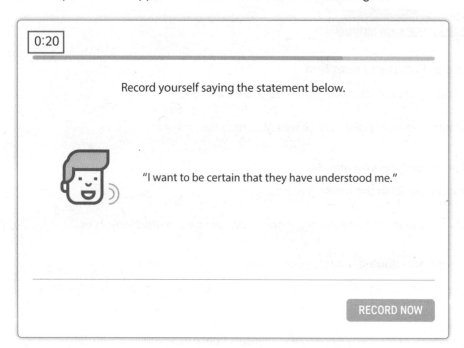

② Before your recording, read the statement out loud first. When you are ready to record, click RECORD NOW and start speaking. A recording sign will appear at the bottom of the screen while you are recording.

③ When you have finished recording, click NEXT to go to the next question. The next question will automatically appear when the time expires.

II. Strategies and Study Tips

Strategy 1. Determine Your Strategy

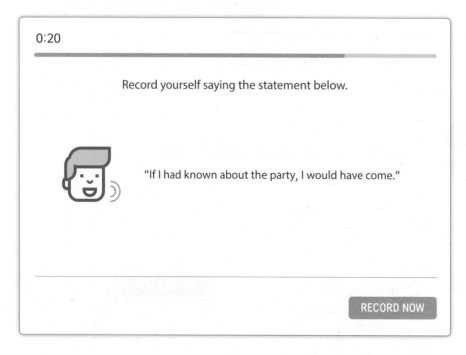

STEP 1 Read aloud

Read the statement aloud first before starting your recording.

If I had known about the party, I would have come.

STEP 2 Check the scoring points

There are 4 scoring points you need to check: pronunciation, stress, linking sounds, and pauses.

① Pronunciation: *had known, would have*

② Stress: stress key words → *If I had known about the party, I would have come.*

③ Linking sounds: *If I had known about the party, I would have come.*

④ Pauses: pause after comma → *If I had known about the party, ∨ I would have come.*

STEP 3 Record with confidence

While thinking about the meaning of the sentence, record it in a loud, confident voice.

If I had known about the party, ∨ I would have come.

Strategy 2. **Improve Your Delivery**

Pronunciation

Because this question type is intended to measure the test taker's delivery in speaking, it is important to understand the basics of English pronunciation. Practice your pronunciation so that you can read without panicking even when a sentence contains unfamiliar or confusing words.

- **ph /f/**

'ph' sounds like /f/ not /p/.

philosophy	/fɪlɑ́:səfi/
phoenix	/fí:nɪks/
choreography	/kɔ̀riɑ́grəfi/

- **Difficult English words to pronounce**

almond	/ɑ́:mənd/
February	/fébruèri/
candidate	/kǽndidèit, kǽndidət/
choir	/kwaiər/
clothes	/klouðz, klouz/
cupboard	/kΛbərd/
hierarchy	/háiərɑ̀:rki/
rural	/rúərəl/
salmon	/sǽmən/
sixth	/siksθ/
Southern	/sΛðərn/
squirrel	/skwə́:rəl/
Wednesday	/wénzdei/
women	/wímin/

Stress

Stress is as important as pronunciation when speaking in English.

- **Stress nouns and verbs**

Generally, nouns and verbs convey the key message of a sentence.

If you need help getting another job, I'll help you with that.

- **Stress words to emphasize the meaning**

Read aloud the words that clarify the meaning of a sentence.

No doubt, he will trade his one and only car for a new one.

Linking sounds

Linking sounds mean that different words come together to sound like one word. Linking sounds make sentences sound more fluent, leaving out unnecessary pauses or extra meaningless sounds. Therefore, linking sounds are important to make your English pronunciation sound more natural. There are several basic principles of linking sounds.

• **Blending**

Blending occurs when one sound moves into another smoothly.

come in → 'me' and 'in' blend together to sound like 'min'

• **Changing sounds**

Some linking sounds are changed into a totally new sound. This happens when either 'd' or 't' comes before 'y'.

want you → 't' and 'y' merge to sound like 'ch'

• **Double sounds**

Double sounds occur when a word finishes with a consonant and the next word begins with the same consonant. There is no pause between the consonants, and only one consonant is pronounced longer.

social life → only one 'l' is pronounced longer

Pauses

Short pauses make your message clear and easy to understand.

• **After commas**

Pause after each comma in a sentence.

My favorite dishes are fish and chips, ∨ tomato pasta, ∨ and chicken noodle soup.

• **When the subject is long**

When a sentence has a long subject, it is natural to have a short pause after the subject.

The books on the left side of the shelf ∨ are for older students.

• **In front of "that" clauses**

Because "that" clauses are usually additional explanations, it is natural to have a short pause in front of them.

The librarian has to come up with a few solutions ∨ that will be helpful for students.

Strategy 3. **Study for Your Target Score**

For DET 100+ Scores

• **Focus on the 4 scoring points**

- Focus on the scoring points (pronunciation, stress, linking sounds, and pauses) to improve your delivery.
- Record yourself and listen to the audio. You can catch mistakes and see which sounds you need to work on.

• **Speak with confidence**

- Speak loudly and clearly so that the AI scoring system can easily understand what you say.
- Remember that speaking confidently will help you sound like you are fluent in English.

• **Do not stress the word if you are unsure**

- If you are unsure whether or not you should add stress, it is better to reduce risk by not adding stress to difficult or unfamiliar words.
- Stress the words that you know accurately to show off your skills.

For DET 120+ Scores

• **Focus on using linking sounds to emphasize fluency**

- Focus on reading the sentence using linking sounds, as they make your speech sound more fluent.
- Do not read the sentence too slowly if you are aiming for a higher score.

• **Do not speak in a rush even if a long sentence appears**

- As the difficulty level increases, longer sentences appear. Do not rush or panic but read them at the same pace as short sentences.
- If a long sentence appears, quickly scan the sentence for difficult words and places to pause. Make sure that you have enough time to speak.

• **Pause after a long subject**

- Think about the meaning of the long subject before you read aloud.
- Add a short pause after the long subject (usually located before a verb).

Level 1 Question [1]

0:20

Record yourself saying the statement below.

"I'd like to go abroad someday."

RECORD NOW

How to Answer the Question

STEP 1 Read aloud

Read the statement aloud first before starting your recording.

I'd like to go abroad someday.

STEP 2 Check the scoring points

There are 4 scoring points you need to check: pronunciation, stress, linking sounds, and pauses.

① Pronunciation: *abroad*

② Stress: *I'd like to go abroad someday.*

③ Linking sounds: *go⌢abroad*

④ Pauses: pause at the last modifier where meaning is added

→ *I'd like to go abroad* ∨ *someday.*

STEP 3 Record with confidence

Thinking about the meaning of the sentence, record it in a loud, confident voice.

I'd like to go⌢abroad ∨ *someday.*

Level 1 Question [2]

0:20

Record yourself saying the statement below.

"I want to be certain that they have understood me."

RECORD NOW

How to Answer the Question

STEP 1   Read aloud

Read the statement aloud first before starting your recording.

I want to be certain that they have understood me.

STEP 2   Check the scoring points

There are 4 scoring points you need to check: pronunciation, stress, linking sounds, and pauses.

① Pronunciation: *certain / have understood*

② Stress: *I want to be certain that they have understood me.*

③ Linking sounds: *want to / have understood*

④ Pauses: pause in front of a "that" clause
→ *I want to be certain ∨ that they have understood me.*

STEP 3   Record with confidence

Thinking about the meaning of the sentence, record it in a loud, confident voice.

I want to be certain ∨ that they have understood me.

Level 2 Question [1]

0:20

Record yourself saying the statement below.

"They received land, seed, livestock, and other items to develop."

RECORD NOW

STEP 1 Read aloud

Read the statement aloud first before starting your recording.

They received land, seed, livestock, and other items to develop.

STEP 2 Check the scoring points

There are 4 scoring points you need to check: pronunciation, stress, linking sounds, and pauses.

① Pronunciation: *received / items*

② Stress: *They received land, seed, livestock, and other items to develop.*

③ Linking sounds: *and other items*

④ Pauses: pause after comma
   → *They received land, ∨ seed, ∨ livestock, ∨ and other items to develop.*

STEP 3 Record with confidence

Thinking about the meaning of the sentence, record it in a loud, confident voice.

They received land, ∨ seed, ∨ livestock, ∨ and other items to develop.

Level 2 Question [2]

0:20

Record yourself saying the statement below.

"People take risks that society will support them, without knowing for sure that it will."

RECORD NOW

How to Answer the Question

STEP 1 Read aloud

Read the statement aloud first before starting your recording.

People take risks that society will support them, without knowing for sure that it will.

STEP 2 Check the scoring points

There are 4 scoring points you need to check: pronunciation, stress, linking sounds, and pauses.

① Pronunciation: *risks / society*

② Stress: *People take risks that society will support them, without knowing for sure that it will.*

③ Linking sounds: *support them / that it*

④ Pauses: pause in front of a "that" clause; pause after comma
→ *People take risks ∨ that society will support them, ∨ without knowing for sure that it will.*

STEP 3 Record with confidence

Thinking about the meaning of the sentence, record it in a loud, confident voice.

People take risks ∨ that society will support them, ∨ without knowing for sure that it will.

0:20

Record yourself saying the statement below.

"The wealth of seafood available on and off the coasts provided the earliest settlers with their sustenance."

RECORD NOW

How to Answer the Question

STEP 1 **Read aloud**

Read the statement aloud first before starting your recording.

The wealth of seafood available on and off the coasts provided the earliest settlers with their sustenance.

STEP 2 **Check the scoring points**

There are 4 scoring points you need to check: pronunciation, stress, linking sounds, and pauses.

① Pronunciation: *wealth / settlers / sustenance*

② Stress: *The wealth of seafood available on and off the coasts provided the earliest settlers with their sustenance.*

③ Linking sounds: *wealth of / seafood available / on and off*

④ Pauses: pause after the long subject; pause at the last modifier where meaning is added
   → *The wealth of seafood available on and off the coasts ∨ provided the earliest settlers ∨ with their sustenance.*

STEP 3 **Record with confidence**

Thinking about the meaning of the sentence, record it in a loud, confident voice.

The wealth of seafood available on and off the coasts ∨ provided the earliest settlers ∨ with their sustenance.

Level 3 Question [2]

0:20

Record yourself saying the statement below.

 "But as the field of genetics continued to develop, those views became less tenable."

RECORD NOW

How to Answer the Question

STEP 1 Read aloud

Read the statement aloud first before starting your recording.

But as the field of genetics continued to develop, those views became less tenable.

STEP 2 Check the scoring points

There are 4 scoring points you need to check: pronunciation, stress, linking sounds, and pauses.

① Pronunciation: *genetics / tenable*

② Stress: *But as the field of genetics continued to develop, those views became less tenable.*

③ Linking sounds: *but̂ as / field̂ of genetics*

④ Pauses: pause after comma
  → *But as the field of genetics continued to develop,* ∨ *those views became less tenable.*

STEP 3 Record with confidence

Thinking about the meaning of the sentence, record it in a loud, confident voice.

But̂ as the field̂ of genetics continued to develop, ∨ *those views became less tenable.*

Write About the Photo

I. All About the Question Type

Key Points

- Write at least one sentence to describe the image on the screen
- Duration: 1 minute
- Around 3 questions of this question type appear as the 5~7th questions

Which Subscores are Assessed

- Production: Ability to <u>write</u> and speak
- Literacy: Ability to read and <u>write</u>

How the Question is Presented

① The question will appear on the screen when the timer begins.

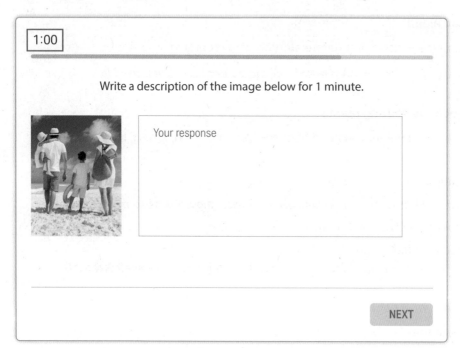

② Look at the image and identify the main subject and background. Write one or more sentences.

③ When you have finished writing, click NEXT to go to the next question. The next question will automatically appear when the time expires.

II. Strategies and Study Tips

Strategy 1. Determine Your Strategy

STEP 1 Write a sentence describing the overall image

As your first sentence, capture the big picture of the photograph by describing the main person/animal/thing.

(Example) This is a photograph of an old man and an old woman with hats on.

STEP 2 Add 1 or 2 sentences describing the details

Add 1 or 2 more sentences that describe the subject's behavior/state or background.

(Example) In detail, they are leaning against each other's shoulders and looking towards a beach.

STEP 3 Proofread and add expressions

If you finish typing before the time limit, check for any grammar or spelling mistakes and see if you can add more expressions.

(Example) This is a photograph of an old man and an old woman with hats on. In detail, they are leaning against each other's shoulders and looking towards a beach and the blue ocean.

Strategy 2. Memorize Essential Expressions

Expressions for location

One way to describe the background is by describing the location. If you practice different ways to express locations, you will be able to write more than one sentence for any given image without any trouble. Use the following expressions, keeping in mind where the main subject is located from the center of the image.

Back	in the background at the back	
Front	in the foreground at the front	
Side	next to ~ right next to ~ on the left/right side	
Additional expressions	in the (left/right/top/bottom) corner above ~ below ~	

Expressions for weather

Another way to describe the background is by describing the weather.

Basic sentence for describing weather	It looks like it is + expression for weather	
Clear/warm weather	bright sunny warm with a clear sky	
Cloudy/cold weather	cloudy foggy gloomy chilly bitterly cold	
Rain/snow	drizzling pouring snowing	

Expressions for people

Most images have people in them, so it is important to learn a variety of expressions to describe people. You should note the characteristics of people, such as their facial expression, age, clothes, behavior, etc., and use appropriate expressions for each situation.

Number of people	one person several people two/three/four people a group of people a crowd (Example) This is a photograph of a group of people in front of a big gate.	 crowd
Age	young old infant toddler child teenager middle-aged in his/her (early/mid-/late) 20s/30s/40s/50s (Example) This is a photograph of a teenager and a woman in her late 40s.	 infant toddler
Facial expression	delighted relaxed confused exhausted depressed frightened nervous upset (Example) This is a photograph of an upset child with her mother.	 depressed upset

Hair	short hair long hair bald head wavy hair curly hair straight hair spiky hair in a bun with braids in a ponytail black/brown/blonde/grey hair (Example) In detail, the middle-aged man on the left side has a bald head.	braid ponytail
Clothes	T-shirt shirt cardigan coat jacket trousers shorts dress skirt shoes boots tight/loose long-sleeved/short-sleeved (Example) In detail, the toddler is wearing a short-sleeved T-shirt and blue shorts.	cardigan short-sleeved shirt
Behavior	walking/jogging/running/driving/riding chatting with (sb)/having a discussion with (sb)/laughing/having a good time standing still/lying down/sitting on + (location) (Example) In detail, the teenagers are chatting with one another, sitting on a bench.	standing still lying down

Strategy 3. **Study for Your Target Score**

For DET 100+ Scores

• **Write at least two sentences**

- You should describe the image in one or more sentences, so always practice writing at least two sentences.
- Write one sentence describing the most noticeable subject in the image and another describing the background.

• **Memorize the expressions for describing images**

- Familiarize yourself with the expressions for describing images and practice using them.
- Use basic sentence structures in order to describe the image within 60 seconds.

For DET 120+ Scores

• **Write three or more sentences**

- If you are aiming for a higher score, explaining in detail is more important than simply giving a list of basic things.
- Write a total of three sentences, including the most noticeable subject, the behavior or state of the subject, and the background of the image.

• **Use adjectives and adverbs**

- Improve your sentences by using various adjectives and adverbs.
- Memorize the synonyms of adjectives and adverbs to expand your vocabulary.

III. Exercise Questions by Level

Level 1 Question

How to Answer the Question

STEP 1 **Write a sentence describing the overall image**

As your first sentence, capture the big picture of the photograph by describing the main person/animal/thing.

This is a photograph of a tall woman with a blue winter coat.

STEP 2 **Add 1 or 2 sentences describing the details**

Add 1 or 2 more sentences that describe the subject's behavior/state or background.

In detail, she is standing still. In the background, there are several trees.

STEP 3 **Proofread and add expressions**

If you finish typing before the time limit, check for any grammar or spelling mistakes and see if you can add more expressions.

This is a photograph of a tall woman with a blue winter coat. In detail, she is standing still. In the background, there are several trees and brick buildings.

Level 2 Question

```
1:00
─────────────────────────────────────

          Write a description of the image below for 1 minute.

  ┌────────────┐   ┌─────────────────────────────────────────┐
  │            │   │ Your response                           │
  │            │   │                                         │
  │   [photo]  │   │                                         │
  │            │   │                                         │
  │            │   │                                         │
  └────────────┘   └─────────────────────────────────────────┘


  ──────────────────────────────────────────────────────────

                                              ┌──────────┐
                                              │   NEXT   │
                                              └──────────┘
```

How to Answer the Question

STEP 1 Write a sentence describing the overall image

As your first sentence, capture the big picture of the photograph by describing the main person/animal/thing.

This is a photograph of a young child and a small orange cat.

STEP 2 Add 1 or 2 sentences describing the details

Add 1 or 2 more sentences that describe the subject's behavior/state or background.

In detail, she is writing something in her book with her pencil. In front of her, the cat is staring at her book to see what she is writing.

STEP 3 Proofread and add expressions

If you finish typing before the time limit, check for any grammar or spelling mistakes and see if you can add more expressions.

This is a photograph of a young child with braids and a small brown cat. In detail, she is writing something in her book with her pencil. In front of her, the cat is staring down at her book to see what she is writing.

Level 3 Question

1:00

Write a description of the image below for 1 minute.

Your response

NEXT

How to Answer the Question

STEP 1 **Write a sentence describing the overall image**

As your first sentence, capture the big picture of the photograph by describing the main person/animal/thing.

This is a photograph of a couple and their child working together in nice weather.

STEP 2 **Add 1 or 2 sentences describing the details**

Add 1 or 2 more sentences that describe the subject's behavior/state or background.

In detail, the child is using a tractor to pull some bales of hay. On the left side, the child's mother is wearing a red T-shirt and looking at her child to check that he is driving the tractor safely.

STEP 3 **Proofread and add expressions**

If you finish typing before the time limit, check for any grammar or spelling mistakes and see if you can add more expressions.

This is a photograph of a couple and their child working together in nice weather. In detail, the child is using a tractor to pull some bales of hay. On the left side, the child's mother is wearing a red T-shirt and looking at her child to check that he is driving the tractor safely. In the top corner, the child's father is wearing a hat to protect himself from the sun.

Speak About the Photo

I. All About the Question Type

Key Points

- Talk about an image that appears on the screen
- Preparation time: 20 seconds
- Duration: You need to speak for a minimum of 30 seconds and a maximum of 90 seconds
- Only 1 question of this question type appears usually as the 32nd question

Which Subscores are Assessed

- Production: Ability to write and <u>speak</u>
- Conversation: Ability to listen and <u>speak</u>

How the Question is Presented

① The question will appear on the screen when the 20-second timer begins.

② The recording begins automatically after the preparation time.

③ Speak for a minimum of 30 seconds and a maximum of 90 seconds. When you have finished speaking, click NEXT to go to the next question. The next question will automatically appear when the time expires.

II. Strategies and Study Tips

Strategy 1. Determine Your Strategy

STEP 1 Identify the main points of the image

During the 20 seconds of preparation time, identify two to three important points of the main subject and background of the image.

Father in yellow T-shirt and a hat / three children

This is a picture of a family on a farm. In detail, I can see that the father is in a yellow T-shirt and a hat. On top of that, he has three children with him.

STEP 2 Tell a story using details

Tell a detailed story by elaborating on the situation depicted in the image.

In the picture, the father is holding two shovels. From this, I can infer that they are about to start working. On top of that, the picture depicts one child hiding behind his father. This clearly shows that he is too shy to take a picture.

STEP 3 **Pay attention to your delivery**

Describe the image for at least 30 seconds, focusing on your pronunciation and speaking in a clear voice to deliver your ideas efficiently.

This is a picture of a family on a farm. In detail, I can see that the father is in a yellow T-shirt and a hat. On top of that, he has three children with him. In the picture, the father is holding two shovels. From this, I can infer that they are about to start working. On top of that, the picture depicts one child hiding behind his father. This clearly shows that he is too shy to take a picture.

Strategy 2. **Use Sentence Starters**

Sentence starters for describing the overall image

The main subject of the image can vary each time, but the fact that you have to describe one image stays the same. Thus, use the following sentence starters to describe the overall image in the first sentence of your response.

• **This is a picture of** + noun

(Example) *This is a picture of a man standing with his daughter.*

• **The picture depicts** + noun

(Example) *This picture depicts a firefighter working with his co-workers.*

• **In this picture, I can see** + noun

(Example) *In this picture, I can see two colorful birds flying in the air.*

• **In the picture, the main subject is** + noun

(Example) *In the picture, the main subject is a couple and their child cooking together in the kitchen.*

Sentence starters for telling a story

If you go beyond simply describing a picture and try to tell a story about what could be happening in the picture, you will get a higher score. Thus, use the following sentence starters to make an inference or give your opinion, connecting your ideas with the first sentence.

• **From this, I can tell that**

(Example) *From this, I can tell that the woman is angry at her child.*

- **This clearly shows that**

(Example) *This clearly shows that it is his first day at work.*

- **Therefore, it is obvious that**

(Example) *Therefore, it is obvious that the weather is very hot and humid.*

- **It looks like**

(Example) *It looks like the people in the left corner are celebrating the child's birthday.*

- **From the photo, I/we can infer that**

(Example) *From the photo, we can infer that it was a long day for them.*

Basic template

Do not describe items randomly in the picture, but do plan in advance in which order you would like to describe them. The template below is intended to help you organize your answer and speak fluently for at least 30 seconds.

- **This is a picture of** + the main subject

- **In detail, I can see that** + the main subject + detailed description (facial expressions, clothes, hair, etc.)

- **On top of that,** + description of the main subject's behavior

- **From this, I can infer that** + inference from the background

- **And in the background,** + description of the background

- **This clearly shows that** + inference from the background

> **Tip**
>
> Question Type 5 and Question Type 6 are similar in terms that both require you to describe a photo, but there are some differences.
>
> | | Question Type 5 | Question Type 6 |
> |---|---|---|
> | **Answer Type** | Writing | Speaking |
> | **Preparation Time** | Not given | 20 seconds |
> | **Answer Time** | 1 minute (at least one sentence) | 1 minute and 30 seconds (at least 30 seconds) |
> | **Number of Questions** | 3 questions (usually appear in Question 5-7) | 1 question (usually appears in Question 32) |

Strategy 3. **Study for Your Target Score**

For DET 100+ Scores

• **Memorize the basic template**

- Memorize the basic template, keeping in mind the different patterns for describing an image.
- Practice using the template until you can speak with a natural tone and accurate pronunciation.

• **Memorize basic expressions for appearance**

- You can easily form one or two sentences if you memorize expressions to describe people's facial expressions, clothes, and hair.
- Practice observing the characteristics of people and use them to form full sentences.

• **Speak for at least 30 seconds**

- Set a timer and practice speaking for a minimum of 30 seconds.
- Practice describing the image in at least 6 sentences.

For DET 120+ Scores

• **Add adjectives and adverbs**

- Describe the photo in more detail by using adjectives and adverbs.
- Memorize the adjectives and adverbs used to describe people's facial expressions, clothes, and hair.

• **Tell a story about the photo**

- You can speak close to the 90 second maximum by adding a story to the basic description of the photo.
- Add one or two more sentences that explain the reason behind the subject's behavior or the general mood of the photo.

• **Pay attention to delivery**

- Practice by describing the same image at least three times.
- Practice regularly to improve your delivery and gain confidence.

III. Exercise Questions by Level

Level 1 Question

0:20

Prepare to speak about the image below.

You will have 90 seconds to speak.

RECORD NOW

1:30

Speak about the image below for 90 seconds.

 RECORDING...　　　⊪⏐⏐⏐⊪ıııı　　YOU CAN CONTINUE AFTER 30 SECONDS

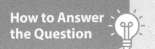
STEP 1 **Identify the main points of the image**

During the 20 seconds of preparation time, identify two to three important points of the main subject and background of the image.

little dog / brown dots / colorful blanket / yellow ball

This is a picture of a little dog with brown dots. In detail, I can see that it is sitting on a colorful blanket. On top of that, it is playing with a yellow ball.

STEP 2 **Tell a story using details**

Tell a detailed story by elaborating on the situation depicted in the image.

From this, I can infer that it is having fun with its owner. And in the background, there is a white wall. This clearly shows that the dog is inside a house.

STEP 3 **Pay attention to your delivery**

Describe the image for at least 30 seconds, focusing on your pronunciation and speaking in a clear voice to deliver your ideas efficiently.

This is a picture of a little dog with brown dots. In detail, I can see that it is sitting on a colorful blanket. On top of that, it is playing with a yellow ball. From this, I can infer that it is having fun with its owner. And in the background, there is a white wall. This clearly shows that the dog is inside a house.

Level 2 Question

0:20

Prepare to speak about the image below.

You will have 90 seconds to speak.

RECORD NOW

1:30

Speak about the image below for 90 seconds.

 RECORDING...   YOU CAN CONTINUE AFTER 30 SECONDS

STEP 1 Identify the main points of the image

During the 20 seconds of preparation time, identify two to three important points of the main subject and background of the image.

blonde woman / man – mustache / stare / fingers crossed

This is a picture of a blonde woman and a man with a mustache. In detail, I can see that they are both staring in the same direction. On top of that, the woman has her fingers crossed with a frowning face.

STEP 2 Tell a story using details

Tell a detailed story by elaborating on the situation depicted in the image.

From this, I can infer that they are watching a sports game and cheering for one team. And in the background, there is another woman staring in the same direction. This clearly shows that they are all enjoying watching a game together.

STEP 3 Pay attention to delivery

Describe the image for at least 30 seconds, focusing on your pronunciation and speaking in a clear voice to deliver your ideas efficiently.

This is a picture of a blonde woman and a man with a mustache. In detail, I can see that they are both staring in the same direction. On top of that, the woman has her fingers crossed with a frowning face. From this, I can infer that they are watching a sports game and cheering for one team. And in the background, there is another woman staring in the same direction. This clearly shows that they are all enjoying watching a game together.

Level 3 Question

0:20

Prepare to speak about the image below.

You will have 90 seconds to speak.

RECORD NOW

1:30

Speak about the image below for 90 seconds.

● RECORDING...

YOU CAN CONTINUE AFTER 30 SECONDS

STEP 1 **Identify the main points of the image**

During the 20 seconds of preparation time, identify two to three important points of the main subject and background of the image.

girl – long hair, T-shirt and jeans / sit – next to sculpture / hold – map

This is a picture of a girl with long hair wearing a T-shirt and jeans. In detail, I can see that she is sitting on a bench with her legs crossed next to a sculpture of a woman. On top of that, she is holding a map in her hands and is looking down at it.

STEP 2 **Tell a story using details**

Tell a detailed story by elaborating on the situation depicted in the image.

From this, I can infer that she is a tourist because the map in her hands looks like a tourist map. Therefore, it is obvious that she is trying to take a photo with the sculpture as part of her trip. And in the background, there are some green trees and grass. This clearly shows that the bench is located near a park.

STEP 3 **Pay attention to delivery**

Describe the image for at least 30 seconds, focusing on your pronunciation and speaking in a clear voice to deliver your ideas efficiently.

This is a picture of a girl with long hair wearing a T-shirt and jeans. In detail, I can see that she is sitting on a bench with her legs crossed next to a sculpture of a woman. On top of that, she is holding a map in her hands and is looking down at it. From this, I can infer that she is a tourist because the map in her hands looks like a tourist map. Therefore, it is obvious that she is trying to take a photo with the sculpture as part of her trip. And in the background, there are some green trees and grass. This clearly shows that the bench is located near a park.

Read, Then Write

I. All about the Question Type

Key Points

- Read a written prompt and write a response with at least 50 words
- Preparation time: 30 seconds
- Duration: You need to write for a minimum of 3 minutes and a maximum of 5 minutes
- Only 1 question of this question type appears usually as the 30th question

Which Subscores are Assessed

- Production: Ability to <u>write</u> and speak
- Literacy: Ability to <u>read and write</u>

How the Question is Presented

① The question will appear on the screen when the 30-second timer begins.

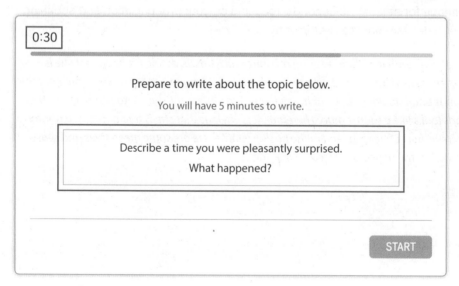

② Write your response for a minimum of 3 minutes and a maximum of 5 minutes. There is no grammar checker or automatic corrector, so pay attention to your grammar, spelling, and punctuation.

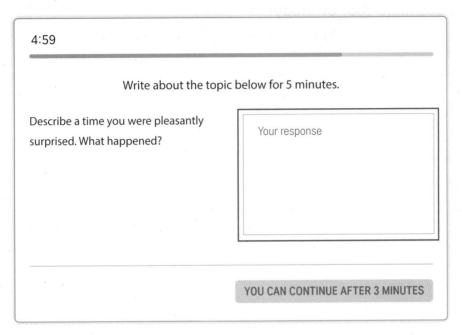

4:59

Write about the topic below for 5 minutes.

Describe a time you were pleasantly surprised. What happened?

Your response

YOU CAN CONTINUE AFTER 3 MINUTES

③ When you have finished writing, click NEXT to go to the next question. The next question will automatically appear when the time expires.

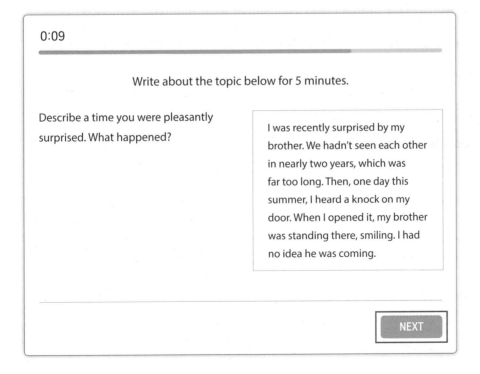

0:09

Write about the topic below for 5 minutes.

Describe a time you were pleasantly surprised. What happened?

I was recently surprised by my brother. We hadn't seen each other in nearly two years, which was far too long. Then, one day this summer, I heard a knock on my door. When I opened it, my brother was standing there, smiling. I had no idea he was coming.

NEXT

Strategy 1. Determine Your Strategy

5:00

Write about the topic below for 5 minutes.

Would you rather attend a job interview in person or by using video conferencing software at home? Why? Give specific reasons for your answer.

> Your response

YOU CAN CONTINUE AFTER 3 MINUTES

STEP 1 **Write a topic sentence**

Identify the keywords in the question and use them to write your topic sentence.

In my perspective, it is more beneficial to attend a job interview by using video conferencing software
   Sentence starter   Your opinion
at home for two major reasons.

STEP 2 **Add details**

Provide supporting ideas by adding explanations and examples.

In my perspective, it is more beneficial to attend a job interview by using video conferencing software at home for two major reasons. First, it is less stressful as an interviewee. Usually, people feel a lot of pressure when being in an environment where the interviewer is asking questions directly in person. However, if I am being interviewed through video conferencing software, I can feel more relaxed when answering questions. Second, video interviews can save time. The companies that I am being interviewed by may be located far from my house and require me to spend a lot of time traveling. However, if I use video conferencing software for interviews, I can just participate in interviews at home.

STEP 3 **End with a concluding sentence**

End with a concluding sentence that summarizes your opinion.

In my perspective, it is more beneficial to attend a job interview by using video conferencing software at home for two major reasons. First, it is less stressful as an interviewee. Usually, people feel a lot of pressure when being in an environment where the interviewer is asking questions directly in person. However, if I am being interviewed through video conferencing software, I can feel more relaxed when answering questions. Second, video interviews can save time. The companies that I am being interviewed by may be located far from my house and require me to spend a lot of time traveling. However, if I use video conferencing software for interviews, I can just participate in interviews at home. To conclude, even though both options may have their advantages, I think that attending a job interview by using video conferencing software is a better option for me.

Strategy 2. Use Sentence Starters

3 types of questions

There are 3 main types of questions that appear on the test.

- **Descriptive:** Describe your personal experience

(Example) *Describe a stressful situation that you managed to get through. What happened?*

- **Explanatory:** Give reasons or methods for the point asked in the question

(Example) *People work for a company because they need to earn money, but what are some other reasons that people choose to work for a company?*

- **Argumentative:** Assert your opinion on the topic

(Example) *People should sometimes do things that they do not enjoy doing. Do you agree or disagree? Why? Give specific reasons for your answer.*

Sentence starters for each type of question

Sentence starters are great writing tools. These words or phrases ease you into your writing, direct the reader's attention to your main ideas, and provide structure for your paragraph.

- **Descriptive**

  - Many people face a situation where + [situation]. In my case, + [description of your experience].
  - It is easy to encounter a situation where + [situation]. I also have a similar personal experience that happened a few years ago.
  - It is true that + [situation]. However, in my experience, [description of your experience].

- **Explanatory**

  - There are several + [key words from the question]. In my view, + [list your ideas].
  - It is true that + [key words from the question]. However, I believe that + [list your ideas].
  - These days, [key words from the question]. The two most prominent ways/factors/implications are + [list your ideas].

- **Argumentative**

  - In my perspective, it is more beneficial to + [your opinion] for two major reasons.
  - I strongly agree/disagree with that statement that + [statement].
  - Some people might prefer to + [other option]. However, it is undeniable that + [your choice].

Strategy 3. **Study for Your Target Score**

For DET 100+ Scores

• **Do not get off topic**

  - Make sure you understand what the question is asking before writing your response.
  - Use the keywords from the question when providing supporting ideas.

• **Check your spelling and grammar**

  - Get into the habit of memorizing the correct spelling of vocabulary words.
  - Always proofread after writing. Make a list of your top 3 grammatical errors and avoid them when writing.

• **Write at least 50 words**

  - Brainstorm two reasons in order to reach the minimum word count.
  - Memorize the basic writing expressions and sentence starters from this book to increase your word count.

For DET 120+ Scores

• **Use varied expressions**

  - Focus on using varied words and expressions rather than using difficult words.
  - Paraphrase to avoid repeating the exact same words or expressions from the question.

• **Write as much as you can**

  - The more you write, the higher your score will be. Practice brainstorming and developing your ideas.
  - Practice writing three to four sentences for each supporting idea.

• **Add details**

  - Add explanations and examples to make your writing more logical and detailed.
  - Use research findings or a personal experience as an example.

III. Exercise Questions by Level

Level 1 Question

0:30

Prepare to write about the topic below.

You will have 5 minutes to write.

> How is the climate in your hometown? How has the climate
> affected your city's culture?

START

5:00

Write about the topic below for 5 minutes.

How is the climate in your hometown?
How has the climate affected your city's
culture?

Your response

YOU CAN CONTINUE AFTER 3 MINUTES

STEP 1 **Write a topic sentence**

Identify the keywords in the question and use them to write your topic sentence.

[Answer to the first question] *Like most cities in my country, my hometown has a temperate climate with four distinct seasons.*

[Answer to the second question] *The climate has affected my hometown's culture in multiple ways. However, the most prominent impact has been on the popularity of the public pool.*

STEP 2 **Add details**

Provide supporting ideas by adding explanations and examples.

Like most cities in my country, my hometown has a temperate climate with four distinct seasons. This means that it is hot and humid in the summer and cold and snowy in the winter. The climate has affected my hometown's culture in multiple ways. However, the most prominent impact has been on the popularity of the public pool. Since it gets so hot in the summer, people need a place where they can stay cool, so everyone goes to the pool.

STEP 3 **End with a concluding sentence**

End with a concluding sentence that summarizes your opinion.

Like most cities in my country, my hometown has a temperate climate with four distinct seasons. This means that it is hot and humid in the summer and cold and snowy in the winter. The climate has affected my hometown's culture in multiple ways. However, the most prominent impact has been on the popularity of the public pool. Since it gets so hot in the summer, people need a place where they can stay cool, so everyone goes to the pool. To conclude, everyone in my hometown goes to the pool in the summer because of the hot weather.

(99 words)

Level 2 Question

0:30

Prepare to write about the topic below.

You will have 5 minutes to write.

More people are living in the city than ever before. What are some reasons that people live in the city?

START

5:00

Write about the topic below for 5 minutes.

More people are living in the city than ever before. What are some reasons that people live in the city?

Your response

YOU CAN CONTINUE AFTER 3 MINUTES

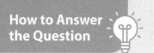
STEP 1 **Write a topic sentence**

Identify the keywords in the question and use these to write your topic sentence.

There are several reasons more people are living in the city than ever before. In my view, most people choose to live in the city because there are more job opportunities and entertainment options.

STEP 2 **Add details**

Provide supporting ideas by adding explanations and examples.

There are several reasons more people are living in the city than ever before. In my view, most people choose to live in the city because there are more job opportunities and entertainment options. In detail, there are many businesses in cities, which means that there are more places to find work. Some examples include large and small companies, shopping malls, restaurants, and cafes. Additionally, there are more places for entertainment in cities. For instance, I live in one of the largest cities in my country. There is a cinema, swimming pool, and bowling club, all within walking distance from my apartment.

STEP 3 **End with a concluding sentence**

End with a concluding sentence that summarizes your opinion.

There are several reasons more people are living in the city than ever before. In my view, most people choose to live in the city because there are more job opportunities and entertainment options. In detail, there are many businesses in cities, which means that there are more places to find work. Some examples include large and small companies, shopping malls, restaurants, and cafes. Additionally, there are more places for entertainment in cities. For instance, I live in one of the largest cities in my country. There is a cinema, swimming pool, and bowling club, all within walking distance from my apartment. To conclude, cities attract many people to live there because they offer better job opportunities and entertainment facilities.

(120 words)

Level 3 Question

0:30

Prepare to write about the topic below.

You will have 5 minutes to write.

> Some people plan their activities during a vacation in advance, while others just decide what to do day by day while on vacation. Which do you prefer? Why? Include specific reasons.

START

5:00

Write about the topic below for 5 minutes.

Some people plan their activities during a vacation in advance, while others just decide what to do day by day while on vacation. Which do you prefer? Why? Include specific reasons.

Your response

YOU CAN CONTINUE AFTER 3 MINUTES

STEP 1 Write a topic sentence

Identify the keywords in the question and use them to write your topic sentence.

It is true that some people prefer to make plans on the spot while traveling. However, in my perspective, it is more beneficial to make plans before a vacation for two major reasons.

STEP 2 Add details

Provide supporting ideas by adding explanations and examples.

It is true that some people prefer to make plans on the spot while traveling. However, in my perspective, it is more beneficial to make plans before a vacation for two major reasons. First, it allows me to not waste time while traveling. For instance, when I was in Italy for vacation two years ago, I already had a plan for every hour of my trip. With this, after visiting each tourist attraction, I was able to direct myself to the next one without wasting any time. Another reason is that you can visit all the places you have wanted to go to. If you do not have a well-made plan in advance, it is highly unlikely that you can visit many places in the limited time period.

STEP 3 End with a concluding sentence

End with a concluding sentence that summarizes your opinion.

It is true that some people prefer to make plans on the spot while traveling. However, in my perspective, it is more beneficial to make plans before a vacation for two major reasons. First, it allows me to not waste time while traveling. For instance, when I was in Italy for vacation two years ago, I already had a plan for every hour of my trip. With this, after visiting each tourist attraction, I was able to direct myself to the next one without wasting any time. Another reason is that you can visit all the places you have wanted to go to. If you do not have a well-made plan in advance, it is highly unlikely that you can visit many places in the limited time period. To conclude, even though making daily decisions while traveling might have some benefits, I think making plans in advance can be more efficient and beneficial.

(153 words)

Read, Then Speak

I. All about the Question Type

Key Points

- Read a written prompt and speak your response
- Preparation time: 20 seconds
- Duration: You need to speak for a minimum of 30 seconds and a maximum of 90 seconds
- Only 1 question of this question type appears usually as the 33rd question

Which Subscores are Assessed

- Conversation: Ability to listen and <u>speak</u>
- Production: Ability to write and <u>speak</u>

How the Question is Presented

① The question will appear on the screen when the 20-second timer begins.

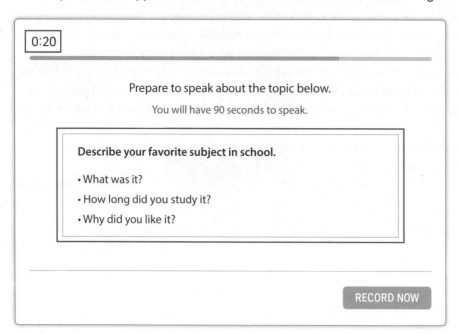

② The recording begins automatically after the preparation time.

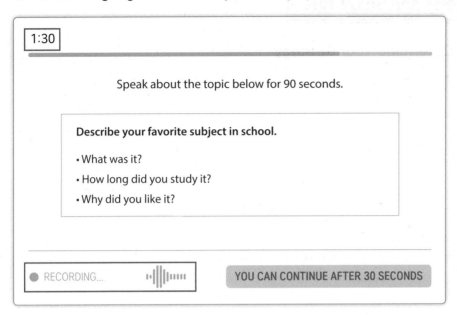

③ Speak for a minimum of 30 seconds and a maximum of 90 seconds. When you have finished speaking, click NEXT to go to the next question The next question will automatically appear when the time expires.

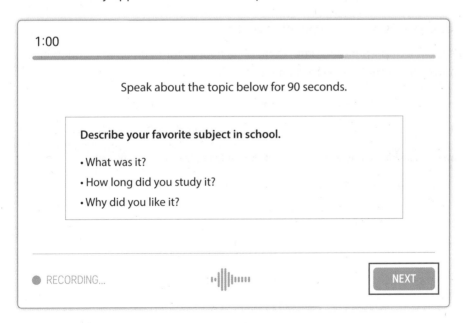

II. Strategies and Study Tips

Strategy 1. Determine Your Strategy

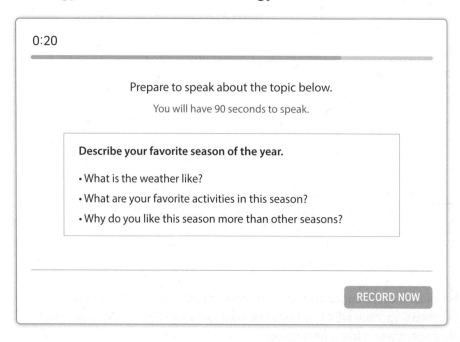

0:20

Prepare to speak about the topic below.

You will have 90 seconds to speak.

Describe your favorite season of the year.

• What is the weather like?

• What are your favorite activities in this season?

• Why do you like this season more than other seasons?

RECORD NOW

STEP 1 **Think of keywords for each specific question**

During the 20 seconds of preparation time, think of keywords for each specific question and brainstorm the details that you want to add.

Describe your favorite season of the year.	▶ spring
What is the weather like?	▶ warm – a little breeze, not hot, not cold
What are your favorite activities in this season?	▶ flower festivals – picnic, walk, pictures
Why do you like this season more than other seasons?	▶ outdoor activities – nice weather

STEP 2 **Identify the tense for each specific question**

Identify the verb and tense for each specific question. Make sure your answers align with the tense.

Describe your favorite season of the year.	▶ spring
What is the weather like?	▶ (present simple) warm – a little breeze, not hot, not cold
What are your favorite activities in this season?	▶ (present simple) flower festivals – picnic, walk, pictures
Why do you like this season more than other seasons?	▶ (present simple) outdoor activities – nice weather

STEP 3 **Create complete sentences**

Use the keywords and details to create complete sentences. Speak clearly and fluently, with confidence.

Personally, my favorite season of the year is spring. To tell you more about this season, it is very warm and nice with a little breeze. There are several activities that you can enjoy in spring, but I believe the best thing to do is going to flower festivals. This is because at the festivals, you can take a walk with your friends or family while looking at colorful and beautiful flowers. It is also nice to take pictures with such scenery. Additionally, the reason why I prefer spring over other seasons is that you can enjoy outdoor activities without having to worry about the weather. For instance, in winter, if it suddenly snows or hails, it is difficult to go for a little walk. On the other hand, in spring, it is highly unlikely that you will be affected by the weather if you want to try an outdoor activity. For these reasons, my favorite season is spring.

Strategy 2. **Know How to Answer the Question**

This question type contains several specific questions that help you answer the main question. In particular, you can use the order of the questions for your own answer template and use words directly from the questions. Practice coming up with your sentences by memorizing the question and answer patterns below.

Question pattern	Answer pattern
Why ~? = What makes ~?	The main reason why ~ = The main reason for ~ is ~
How ~?	~ by ~ing
Who ~?	The person that ~ is ~
What do you think ~?	Personally, I think/believe ~
Do you think ~? Is it ~? How long ~? How much ~?	In my view, the amount of (time/money) for this is ~
What are some ~?	Some of the ~ are ~
Describe something that ~	One thing that ~

(Example)

Describe something that irritates you.	▶ One thing that irritates me is ~
Why does it irritate you?	▶ The main reason why this irritates me is ~
How do you react when someone does this?	▶ When someone does this, I usually react by doing ~
Do you think this irritates others as well?	▶ Personally, I do not think that this would irritate others.

Add details

While you need to speak for a minimum of 30 seconds, aim to speak for the maximum limit of 90 seconds to receive a higher score. In order to do so, avoid short answers. Instead, add details to answer each question fully.

Question	Short Answer (X)	Adding details (O)
Talk about someone in your country who is always in the media.	▶ BTS	▶ BTS – Korean boy band, 7 members
• Why is this person the focus of so much attention?	▶ talented	▶ talented – great singers, perfect choreography
• Is he/she an important person?	▶ yes	▶ yes – very influential, especially in Korea, international fans
• What do you think this person's future will be like?	▶ more successful	▶ more successful – become influential worldwide, release more albums

Someone who is always in the media in my country is BTS. To tell you more about BTS, it is a Korean boy band with seven members. The main reason why this group receives so much attention is because they are very talented. Not only is each member a great singer, but the whole band dances on stage with perfect choreography. In addition, BTS is an important group because the members are very influential in Korea. On top of that, they have become famous in other countries as well, gathering many international fans. Personally, I believe that they will become even more successful and become influential worldwide. I expect them to release more albums that will be international hits. I really hope that I could go to one of their concerts someday.

The speaking section records every moment of your response, including your pauses. Most test takers would normally panic when they run out of ideas or forget what they were about to say, causing them to stumble on their words or be silent. However, you can turn this into an opportunity to show your fluency by using filler words, or words used to fill the pauses in between speaking. Learn the correct pronunciation and tone of the expressions below and use them appropriately during the test.

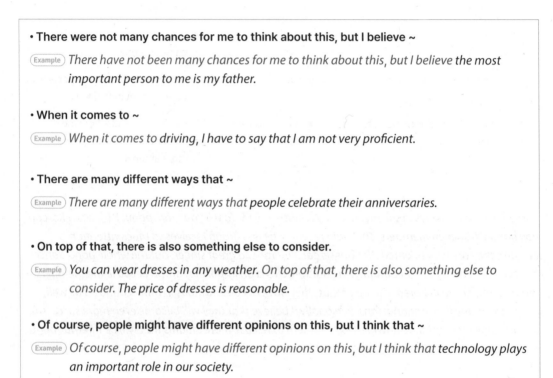

• **There were not many chances for me to think about this, but I believe ~**

(Example) *There have not been many chances for me to think about this, but I believe the most important person to me is my father.*

• **When it comes to ~**

(Example) *When it comes to driving, I have to say that I am not very proficient.*

• **There are many different ways that ~**

(Example) *There are many different ways that people celebrate their anniversaries.*

• **On top of that, there is also something else to consider.**

(Example) *You can wear dresses in any weather. On top of that, there is also something else to consider. The price of dresses is reasonable.*

• **Of course, people might have different opinions on this, but I think that ~**

(Example) *Of course, people might have different opinions on this, but I think that technology plays an important role in our society.*

Strategy 3. **Study for Your Target Score**

For DET 100+ Scores

• **Avoid grammatical errors**

- The simplest way to use correct grammar is to take the sentence structure from the question and use it to make your own sentence. Try to make the best use of the question itself when answering.
- Memorize and practice the filler words provided in this book so that you can use good expressions while avoiding errors.

• **Build on your answer**

- Start with a basic answer that reaches a minimum of 30 seconds.
- When you become confident in coming up with a basic answer, work on improving your time by adding more details.

• **Transcribe your answer**

- Record, listen, and transcribe your answer so that you can check for error patterns visually.
- Add more details and practice speaking your new answer.

For DET 120+ Scores

• **Expand your vocabulary**

- Broaden your range of vocabulary from frequently used words to less common words.
- Refer to the Appendix for synonyms and different word forms of vocabulary words.

• **Use all the time you have**

- Aim to speak close to the 90 second maximum.
- If you find it difficult to add details, memorize and practice filler words to improve your time.

• **Remember to pay attention to your delivery**

- In the speaking section, the delivery of your answer is as important as the content. Practice your pronunciation and intonation, which are the basics of delivery.
- Repeat speaking your answer multiple times until you can speak naturally and clearly.

III. Exercise Questions by Level

Level 1 Question

0:20

Prepare to speak about the topic below.

You will have 90 seconds to speak.

> **Talk about a significant letter that you got from someone.**
>
> • Who wrote it to you?
> • What was it about?
> • How did it make you feel?

RECORD NOW

1:30

Speak about the topic below for 90 seconds.

> **Talk about a significant letter that you got from someone.**
>
> • Who wrote it to you?
> • What was it about?
> • How did it make you feel?

● RECORDING...   YOU CAN CONTINUE AFTER 30 SECONDS

STEP 1 **Think of keywords for each specific question**

During the 20 seconds of preparation time, think of keywords for each specific question and brainstorm the details that you want to add.

Talk about a significant letter that you got from someone.	▶ one letter
Who wrote it to you?	▶ my best friend in high school
What was it about?	▶ celebrate my graduation and friendship since elementary school
How did it make you feel?	▶ touched

STEP 2 **Identify the tense for each specific question**

Identify the verb and tense for each specific question. Make sure your answers align with the tense.

Talk about a significant letter that you got from someone.	▶ (past tense) one letter
Who wrote it to you?	▶ (past tense) my best friend in high school
What was it about?	▶ (past tense) celebrate my graduation and friendship since elementary school
How did it make you feel?	▶ (past tense) touched

STEP 3 **Create complete sentences**

Use the keywords and details to create complete sentences. Speak clearly and fluently, with confidence.

I have received many different letters from people, but let me talk about one significant letter I got in high school. To give you more detail, my best friend in high school wrote it to me. It was about celebrating my high school graduation. On top of that, my friend talked about how our friendship grew since elementary school. When I got the letter from my best friend, I was very touched and felt loved. This is because she mentioned that even though we will be in different colleges, we will never be apart, and our friendship will last forever. For these reasons, the most memorable letter I got was from my best friend in high school.

Level 2 Question

0:20

Prepare to speak about the topic below.

You will have 90 seconds to speak.

Describe how people commute to work.

• How do people commute to work?

• How long do people spend commuting?

• How will commuting change in the future?

RECORD NOW

1:30

Speak about the topic below for 90 seconds.

Describe how people commute to work.

• How do people commute to work?

• How long do people spend commuting?

• How will commuting change in the future?

● RECORDING...   YOU CAN CONTINUE AFTER 30 SECONDS

STEP 1 Think of keywords for each specific question

During the 20 seconds of preparation time, think of keywords for each specific question and brainstorm the details that you want to add.

How do people commute to work?	▶ cars – personal space / public transportation system – X traffic jam – ex) bus, subway
How long do people spend commuting?	▶ average 40 minutes – differ depend on distance
How will commuting change in the future?	▶ bicycle – protect environment – important

STEP 2 Identify the tense for each specific question

Identify the verb and tense for each specific question. Make sure your answers align with the tense.

How do people commute to work?	▶ (present simple) cars – personal space / public transportation system – X traffic jam – ex) bus, subway
How long do people spend commuting?	▶ (present simple) average 40 minutes – differ depend on distance
How will commuting change in the future?	▶ (future tense) bicycle – protect environment – important

STEP 3 Create complete sentences

Use the keywords and details to create complete sentences. Speak clearly and fluently, with confidence.

The way people commute to work differs from person to person, but I believe the two most common ways are using one's car or using public transportation. In my view, the major advantage of driving to work is that you can have your own personal space while going to work. On the other hand, if you take public transportation such as buses or subways, it is less likely that you will experience traffic jams, which in turn, will allow you to arrive on time. The amount of time people spend on commuting may differ depending on the distance from their home to work, but in my opinion, an average person would spend around forty minutes of their time commuting. Even though the two ways of commuting I described have benefits, I suppose that in the future, riding a bicycle will be a more popular way of traveling to work. People are becoming more aware of the importance of protecting the environment. In light of the eco-friendliness of using bicycles, I believe more and more people will decide to use bicycles to commute in the future.

Level 3 Question

0:20

Prepare to speak about the topic below.

You will have 90 seconds to speak.

Discuss how people can increase their earnings.

- Why might a person need to increase their earnings?
- What are some ways that people increase their earnings?
- Is it common for people to increase their earnings?

RECORD NOW

1:30

Speak about the topic below for 90 seconds.

Discuss how people can increase their earnings.

- Why might a person need to increase their earnings?
- What are some ways that people increase their earnings?
- Is it common for people to increase their earnings?

● RECORDING...   YOU CAN CONTINUE AFTER 30 SECONDS

How to Answer the Question

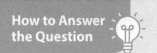

STEP 1 **Think of keywords for each specific question**

During the 20 seconds of preparation time, think of keywords for each specific question and brainstorm the details that you want to add.

Why might a person need to increase their earnings?	▶ increased spending
What are some ways that people increase their earnings?	▶ negotiate salary / change careers
Is it common for people to increase their earnings?	▶ no – a lot of time and effort

STEP 2 **Identify the tense for each specific question**

Identify the verb and tense for each specific question. Make sure your answers align with the tense.

Why might a person need to increase their earnings? (Guess)	▶ (present simple) increased spending
What are some ways that people increase their earnings?	▶ (present simple) negotiate salary / change careers
Is it common for people to increase their earnings?	▶ (present simple) no – a lot of time and effort

STEP 3 **Create complete sentences**

Use the keywords and details to create complete sentences. Speak clearly and fluently, with confidence.

There are several different reasons for people to want more earnings, but I believe the most obvious reason has to be increased spending. Increased spending can result in anything from purchasing more clothes to buying a house. I suppose the desire to spend more money can lead to the need to earn more money. And there are two prominent ways to raise earnings that come to mind. The first and most obvious way is to negotiate your salary with your boss. The second way is to change your career to something else that will ensure you a higher salary. If you ask me if it is common for people to increase their income, my answer would be "no." The main reason for this is that it would require a lot of time and effort. Usually, people already have their own jobs and other commitments. Therefore, in my opinion, it is not easy for them to spend more time on improving themselves for more earnings.

Listen, Then Speak

I. All About the Question Type

Key Points

- Listen to a prompt and speak your response
- You can replay the prompt up to two times (three plays total)
- Preparation time: 20 seconds
- Duration: You need to speak for a minimum of 30 seconds and a maximum of 90 seconds
- 2 questions of this question type appear on your test usually as the 31st and 34th question

Which Subscores are Assessed

- Conversation: Ability to <u>listen</u> and <u>speak</u>
- Production: Ability to write and <u>speak</u>

How the Question is Presented

① The question will appear on the screen when the 20-second timer begins.

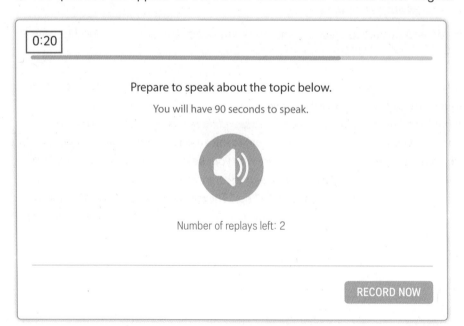

② You can listen to the question two more times by clicking on the speaker button.

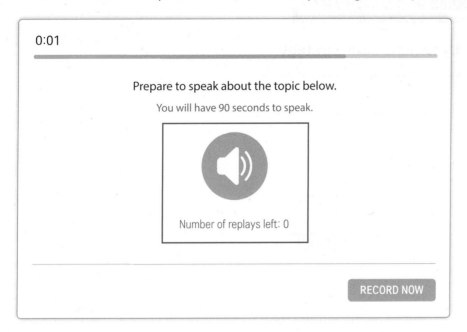

③ Speak for a minimum of 30 seconds and a maximum 90 seconds. Click NEXT to go to the next question. The next question will automatically appear when the time expires.

II. Strategies and Study Tips

Strategy 1. Determine Your Strategy

0:20

Prepare to speak about the topic below.

You will have 90 seconds to speak.

Number of replays left: 2

RECORD NOW

09-01

1:30

Speak about the topic for 90 seconds.

Number of replays left: 0

● RECORDING...

YOU CAN CONTINUE AFTER 30 SECONDS

STEP 1 **Find the keywords in the question**

Listen to the prompt three times and find the keywords in the question.

① First: *someone older*
② Second: *someone older – you admire*
③ Third: *someone older – you admire – how long known and why*

(Question) Think about someone older than you that you admire. How long have you known this person? And why do you admire this person?

STEP 2 **Quickly brainstorm your answer**

During the 20 seconds of preparation time, quickly brainstorm your answer using the keywords.

① Question keywords: *someone older – you admire – how long known and why*
② Answer keywords: *high school teacher – 5 years – learned many lessons*

STEP 3 **Create complete sentences**

Use the keywords to create complete sentences. Make sure you add specific details so that you speak for a minimum of 30 seconds.

Someone older that I admire is my teacher in high school. I have known her for almost five years. From my first class with her in high school, she has been an inspiring figure for me. I remember being amazed by her teaching skills and her passion for her job. Between classes, she would give us advice on our academic and career goals, which became very useful in the future. The main reason why I admire her is that I desire to follow in her footsteps by studying hard to become a teacher.

Strategy 2. Know Common Question Types and Topics

3 types of questions

• **Type 1: In what ways ~ / How should ~ / Discuss ~**

These questions ask you to list the ways or characteristics of the keywords in the question. Discuss two ways or characteristics and add details.

(Example) In what ways can a person show encouragement to a friend or relative who is having some personal difficulties?

> Question keywords: ways – show encouragement – difficulties
> First way: give advice
> Second way: show empathy

• **Type 2: Think about ~ / Talk about ~**

These questions ask you to describe a person, thing, or situation. Generally, there are specific questions that follow after the main question. It is important to answer each question in as much detail as possible.

(Example) Think about someone older than you that you admire. How long have you known this person? And why do you admire this person?

> Main question: someone older that I admire ▸ Answer: boss at work
> Specific question: how long known ▸ Answer: known for 3 years
> Specific question: why admire ▸ Answer: passion for work

• **Type 3: Should ~ ? Why or why not? Do you agree or disagree?**

These questions ask you to state your opinion about the keywords in the question. Brainstorm two reasons for your choice and explain each reason in detail.

(Example) Should parents be held accountable if their children break the law? Why or why not?

> Question keywords: parents held accountable – children break law
> My choice: Yes
> First reason: children are too young to be held accountable
> Second reason: parents should take care of their own children

- **Common topic 1: Describing a person related to you**

influential
inspiring
be famous for
a people person
full of energy
easy-going
courageous
trustworthy
exceptional
versatile
enthusiastic
thoughtful
determined
adventurous
adaptable
humble

- **Common topic 2: Describing a thing related to you**

important
an essential part of my life
meaningful
influential
precious
nice appearance
several functions
handy
paramount

- **Common topic 3: Health and Lifestyle**

eat clean
balanced diet
look after one's health
healthy lifestyle
obesity
health issues
regular exercise
stay in shape

• Common topic 4: Education

primary/secondary/tertiary education
graduate
coursework
retake an exam
qualification
educational institutions
tuition fee
assignments
degree
compulsory education
boarding school
intensive course
sit an exam
online learning
scholarship
gap year

• Common topic 5: Employment and Work

increased education
unemployment rate
internship experience
highly skilled
qualified graduates
specialized skills
workplace
work environment

• Common topic 6: Government

government spending
authority
consensus
regulation
govern
pass a law
guidelines
ballot
autonomy

Strategy 3. Study for Your Target Score

For DET 100+ Scores

• **Understand the question**

  - When you practice listening, interpret the sentences individually right after you hear them.
  - Limit yourself to three chances to listen to the prompt. Practice picking up keywords (usually nouns and interrogatives such as who, why, or which) from the question within three plays.

• **Build on your answer**

  - Familiarize yourself with the common question types and apply the answer patterns for each type (refer to Question Type 8 Strategy 2).
  - Record, listen, and transcribe your answer, then add more details and different expressions.

• **Always pay attention to your pronunciation**

  - You cannot receive a high score no matter how good your ideas are if you convey your ideas poorly, so always remember to speak clearly.
  - Practice shadowing regularly so that you can get familiar with English pronunciation, intonation, and stress.

For DET 120+ Scores

• **Minimize the pauses**

  - Frequent pauses may show a lack of content or fluency, so use filler words (refer to Question Type 8 Strategy 2).
  - Brainstorm ideas for common topics in advance, and practice speaking without hesitation.

• **Use all the time you have**

  - Start with an answer that reaches at least 1 minute.
  - Work on improving your time and aim to speak close to the 90-second maximum.

• **Make a detailed answer to the question**

  - You cannot see the question for this question type, so form the last sentence of your answer using the keywords from the question so that you do not get off topic.
  - Provide details for your answer according to the five Ws and H framework (who, what, when, where, why, and how).

III. Exercise Questions by Level

Level 1 Question

🔊 09-02

0:20

Prepare to speak about the topic below.

You will have 90 seconds to speak.

Number of replays left: 2

RECORD NOW

1:30

Speak about the topic for 90 seconds.

Number of replays left: 0

● RECORDING... YOU CAN CONTINUE AFTER 30 SECONDS

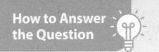
STEP 1 **Find the keywords in the question**

Listen to the prompt three times and find the keywords in the question.

① First: *stunning natural view*
② Second: *stunning natural view – where*
③ Third: *stunning natural view – where and who*

(Question) Talk about the most stunning natural view you have ever seen. Where were you, and who were you with?

STEP 2 **Quickly brainstorm your answer**

During the 20 seconds of preparation time, quickly brainstorm your answer using the keywords.

① Question keywords: *stunning natural view – where and who*
② Answer keywords: *sunset – Sydney – with my best friend*

STEP 3 **Create complete sentences**

Use the keywords to create complete sentences. Make sure you add specific details so that you speak for a minimum of 30 seconds.

The most stunning natural view I have ever seen was the sunset in Sydney. It was 3 years ago, and I still remember the scenery clearly. I was with my best friend in Sydney for vacation. Before the sunset, we had dinner in a nice restaurant by the Opera House. At around 7 o'clock, the sun started going down, and the sky turned into a brilliant red and orange color. We sat on one of the benches next to the Opera House to enjoy the view. We were amazed by how beautiful the sunset was. Therefore, even though I have seen several stunning natural views, the best view was the sunset in Sydney.

Level 2 Question

09-03

0:20

Prepare to speak about the topic below.

You will have 90 seconds to speak.

Number of replays left: 2

RECORD NOW

1:30

Speak about the topic for 90 seconds.

Number of replays left: 0

● RECORDING...   YOU CAN CONTINUE AFTER 30 SECONDS

STEP 1 **Find the keywords in the question**

Listen to the prompt three times and find the keywords in the question.

① First: *military service*
② Second: *military service – compulsory*
③ Third: *military service – compulsory – reasons*

(Question) Should military service be compulsory? Include reasons in your answer.

STEP 2 **Quickly brainstorm your answer**

During the 20 seconds of preparation time, quickly brainstorm your answer using the keywords.

① Question keywords: *military service – compulsory – reasons*
② Answer keywords: *No – 1. individuals need autonomy to choose*
2. passionate people → better outcome

STEP 3 **Create complete sentences**

Use the keywords to create complete sentences. Make sure you add specific details so that you speak for a minimum of 30 seconds.

People might have different opinions on this statement, but in my opinion, military service should not be compulsory. There are several reasons to support my opinion. First, people should have the autonomy to choose to join military services. I believe a nation or society should not have that much control over an individual's life. Plus, if military service is compulsory, those who are not willing also have to participate, which might lead to a lack of motivation. On the other hand, if only those who apply serve in the military, they will be passionate about their work, and this will in turn bring better outcomes. For these reasons, I argue that military service should not be mandatory.

Level 3 Question

09-04

0:20

Prepare to speak about the topic below.

You will have 90 seconds to speak.

Number of replays left: 2

RECORD NOW

1:30

Speak about the topic for 90 seconds.

Number of replays left: 0

● RECORDING...

YOU CAN CONTINUE AFTER 30 SECONDS

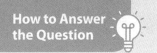
STEP 1 **Find the keywords in the question**

Listen to the prompt three times and find the keywords in the question.

① First: *society lower*
② Second: *society lower – unemployment rate*
③ Third: *society lower – unemployment rate – challenges*

(Question) Describe ways in which society can help lower the unemployment rate. Discuss some of the challenges in doing this.

STEP 2 **Quickly brainstorm your answer**

During the 20 seconds of preparation time, quickly brainstorm your answer using the keywords.

① Question keywords: *society lower – unemployment rate – challenges*
② Answer keywords: *provide education and training – a lot of money*

STEP 3 **Create complete sentences**

Use the keywords to create complete sentences. Make sure you add specific details so that you speak for a minimum of 30 seconds.

There are many different ways in which society can help lower the unemployment rate, but the first way that comes to mind is providing education and training to those who are underqualified. These days, one of the reasons for people not being employed is their lack of education and experience in the field. However, if society provides free education and training for them, more people will be qualified to apply for jobs in a variety of fields. Unfortunately, there could be several challenges in doing this. In fact, it will require too much government spending to provide free services for all underqualified people, and this might not be easy for the government either. Plus, even if more people become qualified through free training and education, there is still the chance that companies will not be prepared to recruit new employees. If this is the case, government spending would have no effect on the unemployment rate. To conclude, even though there are some challenges, I believe that one of the ways that the unemployment rate can be lowered is by providing free education and training.

Interactive Reading

I. All About the Question Type

Key Points

• Read a passage and answer 6 reading questions
• Duration: 7 or 8 minutes for all 6 questions (depending on the question level)
• 2 passages of this question type appear on your test usually as the 24th and 25th question
  - 1 narrative passage
  - 1 informative passage

Which Subscores are Assessed

• Literacy: Ability to <u>read</u> and write
• Comprehension: Ability to <u>read</u> and listen

How the Question is Presented

① A screen that signals the start of the Interactive Reading section will appear for 30 seconds. The directions on the screen will tell you the duration.

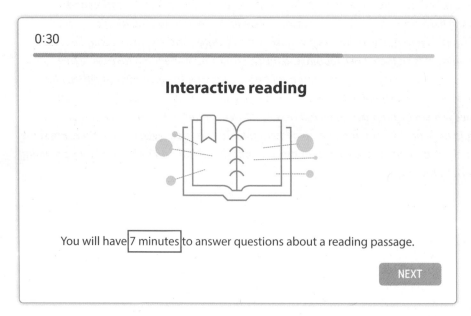

② The first question is Complete the Sentences.

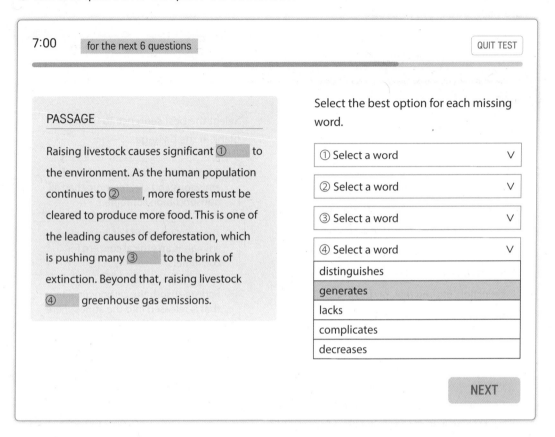

③ The second question is Complete the Passage. The answers to the previous question are filled out in the passage.

4:10   for the next 5 questions   QUIT TEST

PASSAGE

Raising livestock causes significant harm to the environment. As the human population continues to rise, more forests must be cleared to produce more food. This is one of the leading causes of deforestation, which is pushing many species to the brink of extinction. Beyond that, raising livestock generates greenhouse gas emissions.

▬▬▬▬▬▬▬▬

The production of animal products also requires a vast amount of fresh water. Reducing our meat and dairy intake is the best way to limit the environmental impact of raising livestock.

Select the best sentence to fill in the blank in the passage.

- ○ It is the second highest source of emissions and creates more than all transportation combined.

- ○ The cruel treatment of livestock animals is an ethical concern for consumers.

- ○ Forests absorb the carbon dioxide that is released into the atmosphere by human activity.

- ○ The first animals were domesticated for food use around 10,000 B.C.

NEXT

④ The third question is Highlight the Answer. The answer to the previous question is filled out in the passage.

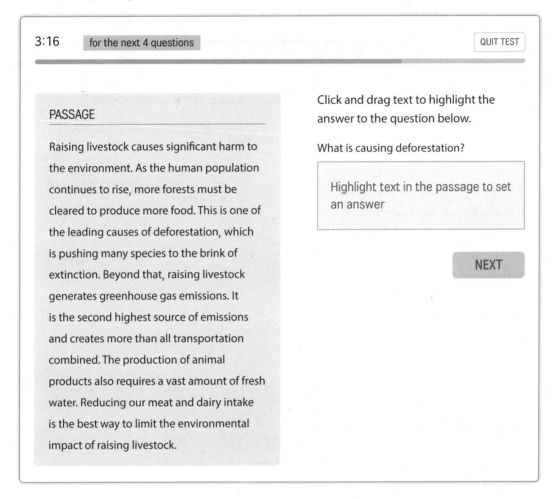

⑤ The fourth question is also Highlight the Answer.

PASSAGE

Raising livestock causes significant harm to the environment. As the human population continues to rise, more forests must be cleared to produce more food. This is one of the leading causes of deforestation, which is pushing many species to the brink of extinction. Beyond that, raising livestock generates greenhouse gas emissions. It is the second highest source of emissions and creates more than all transportation combined. The production of animal products also requires a vast amount of fresh water. Reducing our meat and dairy intake is the best way to limit the environmental impact of raising livestock.

Click and drag text to highlight the answer to the question below.

What effect does raising livestock have on fresh water?

Highlight text in the passage to set an answer

NEXT

⑥ The fifth question is Identify the Idea.

PASSAGE

Raising livestock causes significant harm to the environment. As the human population continues to rise, more forests must be cleared to produce more food. This is one of the leading causes of deforestation, which is pushing many species to the brink of extinction. Beyond that, raising livestock generates greenhouse gas emissions. It is the second highest source of emissions and creates more than all transportation combined. The production of animal products also requires a vast amount of fresh water. Reducing our meat and dairy intake is the best way to limit the environmental impact of raising livestock.

Select the idea that is expressed in the passage.

○ New food production methods are being explored to reduce the environmental impact of raising livestock.

○ While raising livestock causes deforestation, agricultural practices reduce greenhouse gas emissions.

○ Raising livestock damages the environment through harmful emissions and land and resource use.

○ Veganism is the only way to limit the carbon footprint created by the production of animal products.

NEXT

⑦ The last question is Title the Passage.

1:00   for this question

QUIT TEST

PASSAGE

Raising livestock causes significant harm to the environment. As the human population continues to rise, more forests must be cleared to produce more food. This is one of the leading causes of deforestation, which is pushing many species to the brink of extinction. Beyond that, raising livestock generates greenhouse gas emissions. It is the second highest source of emissions and creates more than all transportation combined. The production of animal products also requires a vast amount of fresh water. Reducing our meat and dairy intake is the best way to limit the environmental impact of raising livestock.

Select the best title for the passage.

- ○ Progress Toward a Greener Environment
- ○ The Consequences of Deforestation
- ○ The Impact of Livestock on the Environment
- ○ Switching to a Vegan Diet

NEXT

⑧ After completing both the narrative and informative passage, a screen that signals the end of the Interactive Reading section will appear for 30 seconds.

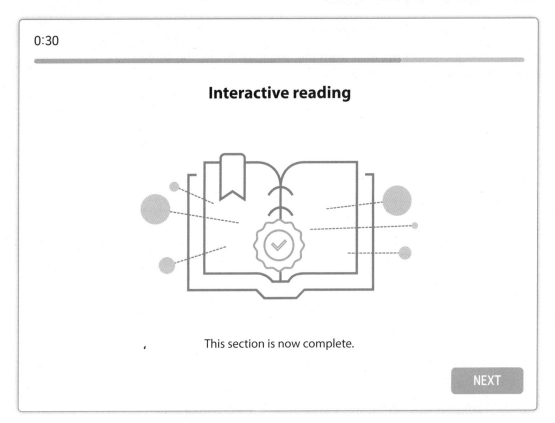

II. Analysis of Each Task

Task 1. Complete the Sentences

- For each blank, select the best word that would complete the sentence
- Number of options per blank: 4 to 5
- Recommended time: Spend 3 minutes (if the duration is 7 minutes) or 4 minutes (if the duration is 8 minutes) on this task
- Strategy: Read the passage carefully, select a word for each missing word, then double-check your answer

Question

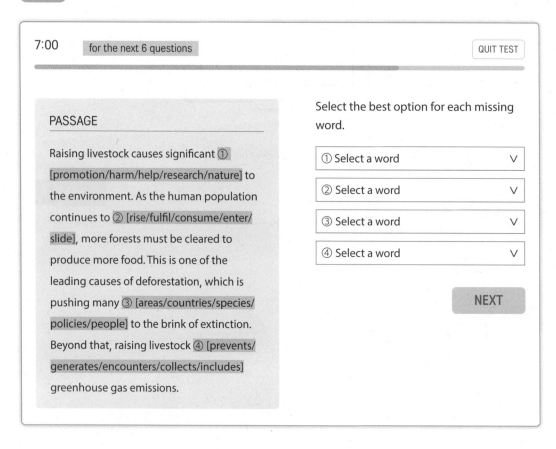

Answers

① harm   ② rise   ③ species   ④ generates

Task 2. Complete the Passage

- Select the sentence that would best fit into the space in the passage
- Number of options: 4
- Recommended time: Spend under 1 minute on this task
- Strategy: Read the sentences before and after the space in the passage, then select a sentence that would fit into the context of the passage

Question

4:10   for the next 5 questions   QUIT TEST

PASSAGE

Raising livestock causes significant harm to the environment. As the human population continues to rise, more forests must be cleared to produce more food. This is one of the leading causes of deforestation, which is pushing many species to the brink of extinction. Beyond that, raising livestock generates greenhouse gas emissions.

_____

The production of animal products also requires a vast amount of fresh water. Reducing our meat and dairy intake is the best way to limit the environmental impact of raising livestock.

Select the best sentence to fill in the blank in the passage.

- It is the second highest source of emissions and creates more than all transportation combined.

- The cruel treatment of livestock animals is an ethical concern for consumers.

- Forests absorb the carbon dioxide that is released into the atmosphere by human activity.

- The first animals were domesticated for food use around 10,000 B.C.

NEXT

Answer

(1) It is the second highest source of emissions and creates more than all transportation combined.

Task 3. **Highlight the Answer**

- Appears as the third or fourth question for each passage
- Highlight the answer to the question that appears on the screen
- Do not highlight too little or too much, but make sure to highlight only the answer to the question
- Recommended time: Spend around 30 to 50 seconds on this task
- Strategy: Use your comprehension of the passage from the previous questions and the keyword from the question to find the answer

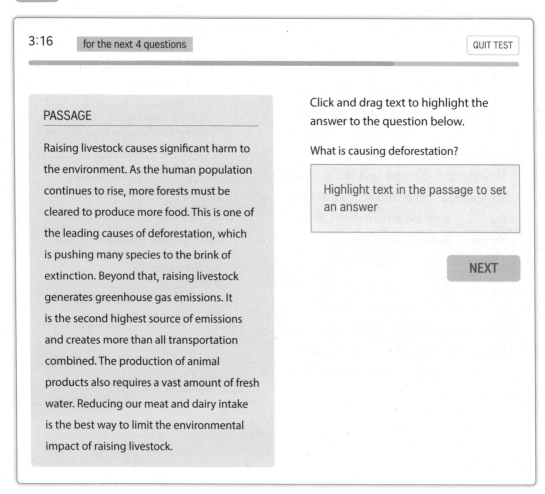

3:16   for the next 4 questions   QUIT TEST

PASSAGE

Raising livestock causes significant harm to the environment. As the human population continues to rise, more forests must be cleared to produce more food. This is one of the leading causes of deforestation, which is pushing many species to the brink of extinction. Beyond that, raising livestock generates greenhouse gas emissions. It is the second highest source of emissions and creates more than all transportation combined. The production of animal products also requires a vast amount of fresh water. Reducing our meat and dairy intake is the best way to limit the environmental impact of raising livestock.

Click and drag text to highlight the answer to the question below.

What is causing deforestation?

> Highlight text in the passage to set an answer

NEXT

Answer

As the human population continues to rise, more forests must be cleared to produce more food.

2:30   for the next 3 questions

QUIT TEST

PASSAGE

Raising livestock causes significant harm to the environment. As the human population continues to rise, more forests must be cleared to produce more food. This is one of the leading causes of deforestation, which is pushing many species to the brink of extinction. Beyond that, raising livestock generates greenhouse gas emissions. It is the second highest source of emissions and creates more than all transportation combined. The production of animal products also requires a vast amount of fresh water. Reducing our meat and dairy intake is the best way to limit the environmental impact of raising livestock.

Click and drag text to highlight the answer to the question below.

What effect does raising livestock have on fresh water?

Highlight text in the passage to set an answer

NEXT

Answer

The production of animal products also requires a vast amount of fresh water.

Task 4. Identify the Idea

- Select the idea that is expressed in the passage
- Number of options: 4
- Recommended time: Spend around 30 seconds on this task
- Strategy: Use the process of elimination to select the idea that is expressed in the passage

Question

1:47 for the next 2 questions   QUIT TEST

PASSAGE

Raising livestock causes significant harm to the environment. As the human population continues to rise, more forests must be cleared to produce more food. This is one of the leading causes of deforestation, which is pushing many species to the brink of extinction. Beyond that, raising livestock generates greenhouse gas emissions. It is the second highest source of emissions and creates more than all transportation combined. The production of animal products also requires a vast amount of fresh water. Reducing our meat and dairy intake is the best way to limit the environmental impact of raising livestock.

Select the idea that is expressed in the passage.

○ New food production methods are being explored to reduce the environmental impact of raising livestock.

○ While raising livestock causes deforestation, agricultural practices reduce greenhouse gas emissions.

○ Raising livestock damages the environment through harmful emissions and land and resource use.

○ Veganism is the only way to limit the carbon footprint created by the production of animal products.

NEXT

Answer

(3) Raising livestock damages the environment through harmful emissions and land and resource use.

Task 5. **Title the Passage**

- Select the best title for the passage
- Number of options: 4
- Recommended time: Spend around 30 seconds on this task
- Strategy: Use the process of elimination to select the idea that is expressed in the passage

Question

| 1:00 | for this question | QUIT TEST |

PASSAGE

Raising livestock causes significant harm to the environment. As the human population continues to rise, more forests must be cleared to produce more food. This is one of the leading causes of deforestation, which is pushing many species to the brink of extinction. Beyond that, raising livestock generates greenhouse gas emissions. It is the second highest source of emissions and creates more than all transportation combined. The production of animal products also requires a vast amount of fresh water. Reducing our meat and dairy intake is the best way to limit the environmental impact of raising livestock.

Select the best title for the passage.

○ Progress Toward a Greener Environment

○ The Consequences of Deforestation

○ The Impact of Livestock on the Environment

○ Switching to a Vegan Diet

NEXT

Answer

(3) The Impact of Livestock on the Environment

III. Exercise Questions

Narrative

PASSAGE

After running her restaurant for a few ① [week/years/day/long/ago], Clara felt that she needed to ② [bring/effort/focus/decide/go] more on treating her customers well. She ③ [created/placed/studied/hired/let] a customer service professional to train her employees so that they would be able to better ④ [serve/see/put/invite/call] patrons of the restaurant. Over several weeks, Clara's staff attended special ⑤ [workers/dishes/goals/interests/meetings] where they ⑥ [bought/developed/continued/brought/talked] their communication skills, patience, and ⑦ [pay/network/hours/respect/uniforms].

Select the best option for each missing word.

① Select a word	⌄
② Select a word	⌄
③ Select a word	⌄
④ Select a word	⌄
⑤ Select a word	⌄
⑥ Select a word	⌄
⑦ Select a word	⌄

NEXT

PASSAGE

After running her restaurant for a few years, Clara felt that she needed to focus more on treating her customers well. She hired a customer service professional to train her employees so that they would be able to better serve patrons of the restaurant. Over several weeks, Clara's staff attended special meetings where they developed their communication skills, patience, and respect. _____

As the restaurant enjoyed more and more repeat business, Clara knew that she had made a wise business choice.

Select the best sentence to fill in the blank in the passage.

- The restaurant workers were unable to treat customers well during busy dinner services.

- They learned that customers were more likely to come back if they received exceptional service.

- She spent time speaking with customers to learn more about their most common complaints.

- Clara opened the restaurant in a crowded downtown area where there were many competitors.

NEXT

PASSAGE

After running her restaurant for a few years, Clara felt that she needed to focus more on treating her customers well. She hired a customer service professional to train her employees so that they would be able to better serve patrons of the restaurant. Over several weeks, Clara's staff attended special meetings where they developed their communication skills, patience, and respect. They learned that customers were more likely to come back if they received exceptional service. As the restaurant enjoyed more and more repeat business, Clara knew that she had made a wise business choice.

Click and drag text to highlight the answer to the question below.

What did Clara do to treat her customers better?

Highlight text in the passage to set an answer

NEXT

PASSAGE

After running her restaurant for a few years, Clara felt that she needed to focus more on treating her customers well. She hired a customer service professional to train her employees so that they would be able to better serve patrons of the restaurant. Over several weeks, Clara's staff attended special meetings where they developed their communication skills, patience, and respect. They learned that customers were more likely to come back if they received exceptional service. As the restaurant enjoyed more and more repeat business, Clara knew that she had made a wise business choice.

Click and drag text to highlight the answer to the question below.

What did Clara's employees learn in their customer service meetings?

Highlight text in the passage to set an answer

NEXT

PASSAGE

After running her restaurant for a few years, Clara felt that she needed to focus more on treating her customers well. She hired a customer service professional to train her employees so that they would be able to better serve patrons of the restaurant. Over several weeks, Clara's staff attended special meetings where they developed their communication skills, patience, and respect. They learned that customers were more likely to come back if they received exceptional service. As the restaurant enjoyed more and more repeat business, Clara knew that she had made a wise business choice.

Select the idea that is expressed in the passage.

- ○ Clara randomly hired a new employee at her restaurant who greatly improved customer service.

- ○ The biggest problem Clara had with her restaurant was the poor customer service skills of her employees.

- ○ Clara realized that improving customer service would be an effective way to improve her restaurant.

- ○ The work quality of Clara's employees improved after she agreed to increase their pay.

NEXT

PASSAGE

After running her restaurant for a few years, Clara felt that she needed to focus more on treating her customers well. She hired a customer service professional to train her employees so that they would be able to better serve patrons of the restaurant. Over several weeks, Clara's staff attended special meetings where they developed their communication skills, patience, and respect. They learned that customers were more likely to come back if they received exceptional service. As the restaurant enjoyed more and more repeat business, Clara knew that she had made a wise business choice.

Select the best title for the passage.

○ Training Tips for Restaurant Staff

○ Clara Improves her Restaurant

○ Common Restaurant Problems

○ Renovating a Restaurant

NEXT

Answers

Complete the Sentences

① years ② focus ③ hired ④ serve ⑤ meetings ⑥ developed ⑦ respect

Complete the Passage

(2) They learned that customers were more likely to come back if they received exceptional service.

Highlight the Answer

She hired a customer service professional to train her employees so that they would be able to better serve patrons of the restaurant.

They learned that customers were more likely to come back if they received exceptional service.

Identify the Idea

(3) Clara realized that improving customer service would be an effective way to improve her restaurant.

Title the Passage

(2) Clara Improves her Restaurant

Informative

PASSAGE

It looks like Canadian geese are ① [moving/ seeing/down/away/attracting] to the suburbs. More and more Americans and Canadians have noticed the noisy birds settling into golf courses, soccer fields, and backyards year-long. Typically, Canadian geese migrate ② [all/some/every/fast/ on] spring. They ③ [see/fly/over/long/ felt] more than 1,500 miles in their iconic V-formations to their nesting grounds in the sub-Arctic. However, this ④ [location/ research/behavior/management/emotion] is becoming less typical for several ⑤ [places/last/flocks/reasons/about]. For one thing, milder winters have made southern regions more hospitable to the ⑥ [residents/ suburbs/buildings/birds/flights].

Select the best option for each missing word.

① Select a word   ∨

② Select a word   ∨

③ Select a word   ∨

④ Select a word   ∨

⑤ Select a word   ∨

⑥ Select a word   ∨

NEXT

PASSAGE

It looks like Canadian geese are moving to the suburbs. More and more Americans and Canadians have noticed the noisy birds settling into golf courses, soccer fields, and backyards year-long. Typically, Canadian geese migrate every spring. They fly more than 1,500 miles in their iconic V-formations to their nesting grounds in the sub-Arctic. However, this behavior is becoming less typical for several reasons. For one thing, milder winters have made southern regions more hospitable to the birds.

_____

They offer plenty of food, access to bodies of water, and protection from both natural predators and hunters. In fact, geese that do not migrate have larger egg clutches and their chicks have longer lifespans.

Select the best sentence to fill in the blank in the passage.

○ Conservation efforts reintroduced captive geese across the northern United States.

○ The birds have also taken residence in Europe and New Zealand.

○ Many people complain about their aggressive nature.

○ In addition, suburban areas are ideal habitats for geese.

NEXT

PASSAGE

It looks like Canadian geese are moving to the suburbs. More and more Americans and Canadians have noticed the noisy birds settling into golf courses, soccer fields, and backyards year-long. Typically, Canadian geese migrate every spring. They fly more than 1,500 miles in their iconic V-formations to their nesting grounds in the sub-Arctic. However, this behavior is becoming less typical for several reasons. For one thing, milder winters have made southern regions more hospitable to the birds. In addition, suburban areas are ideal habitats for geese. They offer plenty of food, access to bodies of water, and protection from both natural predators and hunters. In fact, geese that do not migrate have larger egg clutches and their chicks have longer lifespans.

Click and drag text to highlight the answer to the question below.

What has made southern regions more suitable to Canadian geese?

Highlight text in the passage to set an answer

NEXT

PASSAGE

It looks like Canadian geese are moving to the suburbs. More and more Americans and Canadians have noticed the noisy birds settling into golf courses, soccer fields, and backyards year-long. Typically, Canadian geese migrate every spring. They fly more than 1,500 miles in their iconic V-formations to their nesting grounds in the sub-Arctic. However, this behavior is becoming less typical for several reasons. For one thing, milder winters have made southern regions more hospitable to the birds. In addition, suburban areas are ideal habitats for geese. They offer plenty of food, access to bodies of water, and protection from both natural predators and hunters. In fact, geese that do not migrate have larger egg clutches and their chicks have longer lifespans.

Click and drag text to highlight the answer to the question below.

What makes suburbs attractive places for Canadian geese to live?

Highlight text in the passage to set an answer

NEXT

PASSAGE

It looks like Canadian geese are moving to the suburbs. More and more Americans and Canadians have noticed the noisy birds settling into golf courses, soccer fields, and backyards year-long. Typically, Canadian geese migrate every spring. They fly more than 1,500 miles in their iconic V-formations to their nesting grounds in the sub-Arctic. However, this behavior is becoming less typical for several reasons. For one thing, milder winters have made southern regions more hospitable to the birds. In addition, suburban areas are ideal habitats for geese. They offer plenty of food, access to bodies of water, and protection from both natural predators and hunters. In fact, geese that do not migrate have larger egg clutches and their chicks have longer lifespans.

Select the idea that is expressed in the passage.

○ The Arctic's changing climate has altered the migration patterns of Canadian geese.

○ Canadian geese are frequent nuisances to residents in American and Canadian suburbs.

○ Suburban areas are becoming the permanent homes of Canadian geese.

○ Canadian geese that do not migrate lay more eggs than those that do.

NEXT

PASSAGE

It looks like Canadian geese are moving to the suburbs. More and more Americans and Canadians have noticed the noisy birds settling into golf courses, soccer fields, and backyards year-long. Typically, Canadian geese migrate every spring. They fly more than 1,500 miles in their iconic V-formations to their nesting grounds in the sub-Arctic. However, this behavior is becoming less typical for several reasons. For one thing, milder winters have made southern regions more hospitable to the birds. In addition, suburban areas are ideal habitats for geese. They offer plenty of food, access to bodies of water, and protection from both natural predators and hunters. In fact, geese that do not migrate have larger egg clutches and their chicks have longer lifespans.

Select the best title for the passage.

○ Canadian Geese Settle into Suburban Life

○ Difficult Times for Canadian Geese

○ Geese Rebound from Edge of Extinction

○ How to Deal with Unwelcome Geese

NEXT

Answers

Complete the Sentences

① moving ② every ③ fly ④ behavior ⑤ reasons ⑥ birds

Complete the Passage

(4) In addition, suburban areas are ideal habitats for geese.

Highlight the Answer

milder winters have made southern regions more hospitable to the birds.

They offer plenty of food, access to bodies of water, and protection from both natural predators and hunters.

Identify the Idea

(3) Suburban areas are becoming the permanent homes of Canadian geese.

Title the Passage

(1) Canadian Geese Settle into Suburban Life

Interactive Listening

I. All About the Question Type

Key Points

- Participate in a conversation and answer 2 types of questions
  - Listen and Respond: Around 5 questions
  - Summarize the Conversation: 1 question
- Duration: 4 minutes for all Listen and Respond questions and 75 seconds for Summarize the Conversation
- 2 conversations of this question type appear on your test after the Interactive Reading section
  - 1 conversation between a student and a professor
  - 1 conversation between two students

Which Subscores are Assessed

- Comprehension: Ability to read and listen
- Conversation: Ability to listen and speak
- Production: Ability to write and speak
- Literacy: Ability to read and write

How the Question is Presented

① The character and conversation scenario will appear on the screen. The 4-minute timer will start as soon as you see this screen.

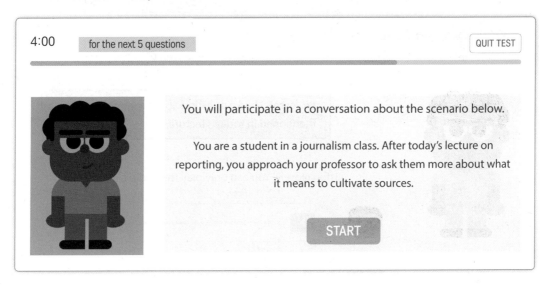

② The first question asks you to "Pick the best option to start the conversation." However, this question may not always appear on the test.

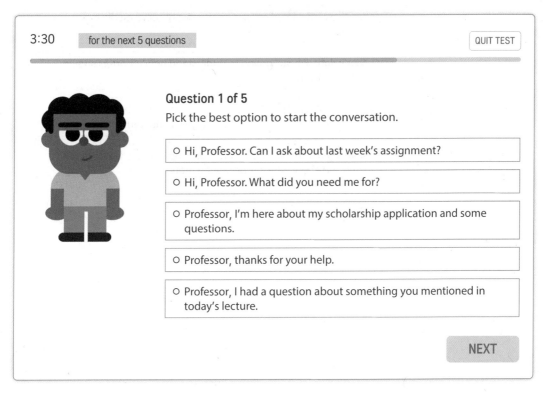

③ You will listen to the audio clip, then select the best response. You can listen to each clip only once, but you can read a transcript of the earlier parts of the conversation. The answers to the previous questions are given in the transcript.

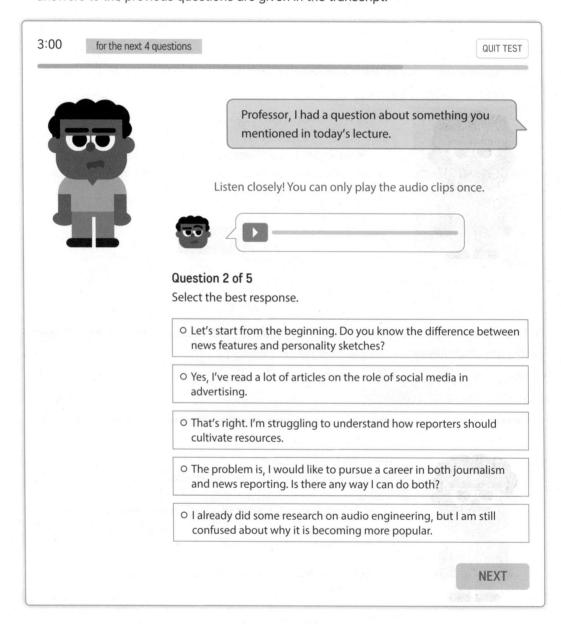

3:00   for the next 4 questions   QUIT TEST

Professor, I had a question about something you mentioned in today's lecture.

Listen closely! You can only play the audio clips once.

Question 2 of 5

Select the best response.

○ Let's start from the beginning. Do you know the difference between news features and personality sketches?

○ Yes, I've read a lot of articles on the role of social media in advertising.

○ That's right. I'm struggling to understand how reporters should cultivate resources.

○ The problem is, I would like to pursue a career in both journalism and news reporting. Is there any way I can do both?

○ I already did some research on audio engineering, but I am still confused about why it is becoming more popular.

NEXT

④ After the Listen and Respond questions, you will write a summary of the conversation you just had. The 75-second timer will start as soon as you see this screen.

1:15

QUIT TEST

Summarize the conversation you just had in 75 seconds.

Your response

NEXT

II. Analysis of Each Task

Task 1. Listen and Respond

- Pick the best option to start the conversation or select the best response
- Number of options: Around 5
- Strategy:
1) Know the common topics: Asking your professor or friend for advice on university programs, future careers, difficulties in class, and other university-related topics
2) Use the process of elimination: Select the option that best fits the conversation
3) Focus on the audio clips: The audio clips are played only once; however, listening to the audio clips does not count towards your time, so stay calm and focused

Question

4:00   for the next 5 questions   QUIT TEST

You will participate in a conversation about the scenario below.

You are a student in a journalism class. After today's lecture on reporting, you approach your professor to ask them more about what it means to cultivate sources.

Question 1 of 5

Pick the best option to start the conversation.

○ Hi, Professor. Can I ask about last week's assignment?

○ Hi, Professor. What did you need me for?

○ Professor, I'm here about my scholarship application and some questions.

○ Professor, thanks for your help.

○ Professor, I had a question about something you mentioned in today's lecture.

NEXT

Answer

(5) Professor, I had a question about something you mentioned in today's lecture.

Task 2. Summarize the Conversation

- Type your summary of the conversation
- Strategy:
  1) Plan ahead: If you finish the Listen and Respond questions before the time expires, spend the remaining time reading and preparing to summarize the conversation
  2) Write at least three sentences: Write one sentence summarizing the scenario, another sentence summarizing the key points of the conversation, and a final sentence summarizing the conclusion
  3) Proofread your writing: If you have time remaining, check your spelling and grammar for any errors

1:15   QUIT TEST

Summarize the conversation you just had in 75 seconds.

Your response

NEXT

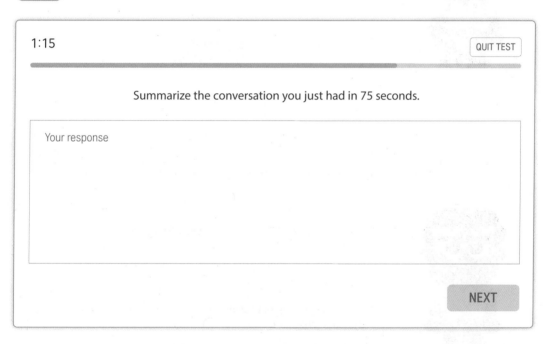

Answer

I was speaking to my professor because I had difficulty understanding the concept of cultivating sources after his lecture. He explained that it is the process of building relationships with people who can provide reporters with valuable information. In the end, he advised me to check out a website for more detailed information.

III. Exercise Questions

Conversation Between a Student and a Professor

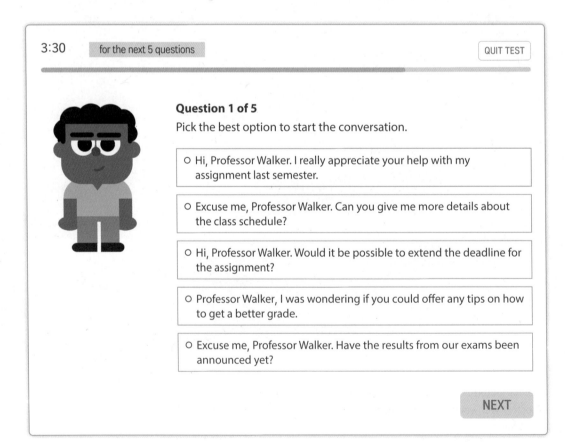

4:00 for the next 5 questions   QUIT TEST

You will participate in a conversation about the scenario below.

You are struggling with one of your classes, and you approach your professor to ask about ways in which you could improve your results this semester.

START

3:30 for the next 5 questions   QUIT TEST

Question 1 of 5
Pick the best option to start the conversation.

○ Hi, Professor Walker. I really appreciate your help with my assignment last semester.

○ Excuse me, Professor Walker. Can you give me more details about the class schedule?

○ Hi, Professor Walker. Would it be possible to extend the deadline for the assignment?

○ Professor Walker, I was wondering if you could offer any tips on how to get a better grade.

○ Excuse me, Professor Walker. Have the results from our exams been announced yet?

NEXT

Professor Walker, I was wondering if you could offer any tips on how to get a better grade.

Listen closely! You can only play the audio clips once.

11-01

Question 2 of 5

Select the best response.

○ That's nice of you to say, but I think I could use some extra help.

○ The main problem I'm having is remembering the names of all the plant structures.

○ Exactly! The work this semester is a lot more complicated than the work we had last year.

○ I'm considering Biology because I love to learn about plants and various biological processes.

○ Yes, that's the topic that I've studied the hardest throughout the semester.

NEXT

 Well, there are a few things you could do. What area are you struggling in the most?

The main problem I'm having is remembering the names of all the plant structures.

◁)) 11-02

Question 3 of 5

Select the best response.

○ I really appreciate you loaning me that textbook. I promise to return it as soon as I'm finished with it.

○ Most of the exam was quite straightforward, but I admit there were a few questions that confused me.

○ I already borrowed all of them from the library, but I'm still having trouble. I need to try a new approach.

○ Well, if you are sure that it's okay, I would love to attend an additional class on the topic.

○ That's a good point. I suppose if I checked some of those websites, I'd gain a better understanding of plant biology.

NEXT

I see. Yes, plant anatomy can be a very tricky topic. The first thing I would suggest is reading the textbooks on the recommended reading list for my class.

I already borrowed all of them from the library, but I'm still having trouble. I need to try a new approach.

🔊 11-03

Question 4 of 5

Select the best response.

- ○ According to the study group schedule, students should meet in one of the meeting rooms in the library.

- ○ That's a great idea! That way, I could learn more and gain experience by actually working within the industry.

- ○ Thanks for the advice, but I don't think I'll have enough time in my schedule to get the essay finished on time.

- ○ I did think about that, but I don't know any of the other students very well, so I'm not confident enough to ask them.

- ○ It's definitely worth considering. I didn't realize that the presentation slides were available to all students.

NEXT

 In that case, have you considered forming a study group with some of your classmates? That could be really helpful.

I did think about that, but I don't know any of the other students very well, so I'm not confident enough to ask them.

🔊 11-04

Question 5 of 5

Select the best response.

- ○ It was an excellent idea. I found it really informative and useful, and it really helped me to boost my grades.

- ○ I'll certainly do my best to meet that deadline. But would it be possible to have a couple of extra days, if necessary?

- ○ I'm glad to hear that! I think it would help a lot of us, not only with our grades, but also by giving us a chance to work together.

- ○ I'm afraid I wouldn't be able to attend the Wednesday session. Would it be possible to switch to Thursday instead?

- ○ Great! Most of the students worked together very well and communicated their ideas clearly. I'd certainly go to another one.

NEXT

I completely understand. Well, you aren't the only student who would benefit from some extra study, so I'll organize some study groups by the end of the week.

I'm glad to hear that! I think it would help a lot of us, not only with our grades, but also by giving us a chance to work together.

The task is complete.

NEXT

Summarize the conversation you just had in 75 seconds.

Your response

NEXT

Answers

Listen and Respond

Question 1 of 5

(4) Professor Walker, I was wondering if you could offer any tips on how to get a better grade.

Question 2 of 5

(2) The main problem I'm having is remembering the names of all the plant structures.

Question 3 of 5

(3) I already borrowed all of them from the library, but I'm still having trouble. I need to try a new approach.

Question 4 of 5

(4) I did think about that, but I don't know any of the other students very well, so I'm not confident enough to ask them.

Question 5 of 5

(3) I'm glad to hear that! I think it would help a lot of us, not only with our grades but also by giving us a chance to work together.

Summarize the Conversation

I was speaking with my professor because I was having problems in his class and wanted to find out how I could improve my grade. He suggested that I read some of the recommended textbooks, but I told him I had already done that and was still having problems. In the end, he said he would organize study groups for the students.

Conversation Between Two Students

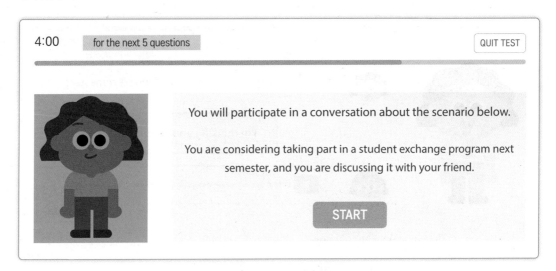

4:00 for the next 5 questions

QUIT TEST

You will participate in a conversation about the scenario below.

You are considering taking part in a student exchange program next semester, and you are discussing it with your friend.

START

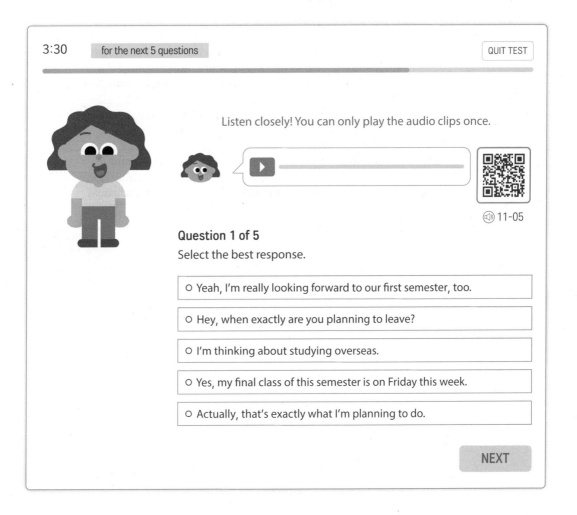

3:30 for the next 5 questions

QUIT TEST

Listen closely! You can only play the audio clips once.

11-05

Question 1 of 5

Select the best response.

- ○ Yeah, I'm really looking forward to our first semester, too.
- ○ Hey, when exactly are you planning to leave?
- ○ I'm thinking about studying overseas.
- ○ Yes, my final class of this semester is on Friday this week.
- ○ Actually, that's exactly what I'm planning to do.

NEXT

 So, do you have any plans for next semester?

I'm thinking about studying overseas.

 11-06

Question 2 of 5

Select the best response.

○ That's what I heard, too. It's a shame there are no spaces left.

○ Really? I'm a bit worried about living in a foreign country, though.

○ I guess you're right. It would be very difficult to adapt to a new culture.

○ Moving here to study was the best decision I've ever made.

○ I am not sure about that. I would have to check my schedule.

NEXT

 That's a great idea! I wouldn't mind doing that as well.

Really? I'm a bit worried about living in a foreign country, though.

  ▶

🔊 11-07

Question 3 of 5

Select the best response.

○ You make a good point. It's not as expensive as I thought.

○ You're right. And it's a great chance to travel around a new country.

○ You're right. The professors there are highly regarded.

○ I agree. It's such an interesting subject to study.

○ Canada? That's amazing! I've always wanted to visit there.

NEXT

 Yeah, I know it's a really big step, but it would be such a rewarding experience. You'd get to meet a diverse range of people and learn about a different culture.

You're right. And it's a great chance to travel around a new country.

🔊 11-08

Question 4 of 5

Select the best response.

○ It's important that you choose a country that you already know a little about. Perhaps you could do some research online.

○ You're totally right. It really helped me to improve my language skills and make a lot of new friends overseas.

○ Yeah, but that's what I'm slightly afraid of. I'm worried that the language barrier will cause me so many problems, and I might not like any of the food.

○ Sure, I'd love it if you came with me! Once you've decided, please let me know and we can begin planning everything together.

○ You make it sound so appealing. I had no idea how many students took part in the exchange program each semester.

NEXT

 And you will have a great opportunity to learn a foreign language and try different foods.

Yeah, but that's what I'm slightly afraid of. I'm worried that the language barrier will cause me so many problems, and I might not like any of the food.

🔊 11-09

Question 5 of 5

Select the best response.

○ That's a great tip. It would be really beneficial to chat with some of our classmates that studied overseas during the previous semester.

○ Perhaps you're right. It might not be the best idea for me and it might have a negative impact on my grades.

○ Okay, thanks for the advice. I'll read it over and try to figure out what the best travel options would be for me.

○ That's a pity. I was really looking forward to getting the opportunity to study somewhere other than my home country.

○ Well, since you enjoyed it so much yourself, I guess I'd be foolish not to give it a shot next year.

NEXT

I appreciate there might be some obstacles, but that's what would make it so exciting. You should speak with some students who have done the exchange before.

That's a great tip. It would be really beneficial to chat with some of our classmates that studied overseas during the previous semester.

The task is complete.

NEXT

Summarize the conversation you just had in 75 seconds.

Your response

NEXT

Answers

Listen and Respond

Question 1 of 5

(3) I'm thinking about studying overseas.

Question 2 of 5

(2) Really? I'm a bit worried about living in a foreign country, though.

Question 3 of 5

(2) You're right. And it's a great chance to travel around a new country.

Question 4 of 5

(3) Yeah, but that's what I'm slightly afraid of. I'm worried that the language barrier will cause me so many problems, and I might not like any of the food.

Question 5 of 5

(1) That's a great tip. It would be really beneficial to chat with some of our classmates that studied overseas during the previous semester.

Summarize the Conversation

I was talking to my friend about studying overseas next semester as part of a student exchange program. She thought it would be a great idea, but I was concerned about problems like food and language. In the end, I decided to speak with other students who have done a similar thing.

Writing Sample

I. All about the Question Type

Key Points

- Read a written prompt and write a response that demonstrates your writing skills
- Your Writing Sample will be available to the universities that receive your results
- Preparation time: 30 seconds
- Duration: You need to write for a minimum of 3 minutes and a maximum of 5 minutes
- Only 1 question of this question type appears usually as the 35th question

Which Subscores are Assessed

- Production: Ability to <u>write</u> and speak
- Literacy: Ability to read and <u>write</u>

How the Question is Presented

① A screen that signals the start of the Writing Sample and Speaking Sample will appear for 30 seconds.

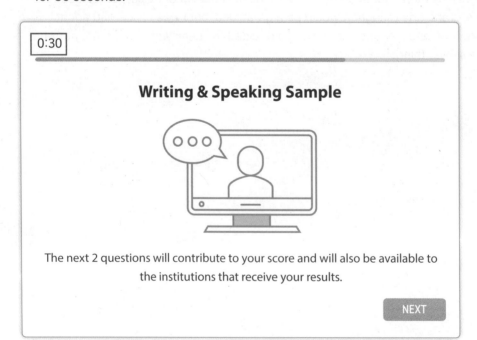

② The question will appear on the screen when the 30-second timer begins.

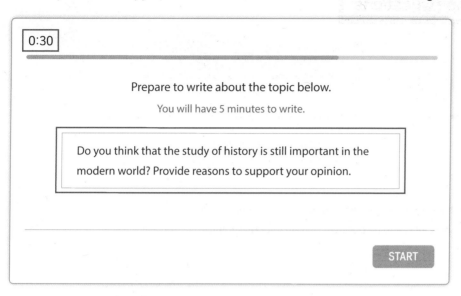

③ Write your response for a minimum of 3 minutes and a maximum of 5 minutes, then submit your response.

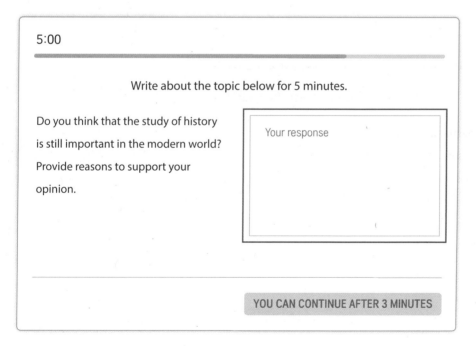

II. Exercise Questions

1

0:30

Prepare to write about the topic below.

You will have 5 minutes to write.

> What do you think it means to be a positive person, and how
> important is it to be positive? Explain your reasoning.

START

5:00

Write about the topic below for 5 minutes.

What do you think it means to be a
positive person, and how important
is it to be positive? Explain your
reasoning.

Your response

YOU CAN CONTINUE AFTER 3 MINUTES

Many people may have different opinions on this, but in my view, being a positive person means not worrying too much, whatever the circumstances. To elaborate on this, a positive person usually interprets challenging situations in the most optimistic way. I can say this because I am an extremely positive person. For instance, when I was in college, I failed an important test. At first, I was very disappointed in myself and felt upset. However, I remembered that failing the test was not the end of the world, and I could make it up on the next exam if I tried my best. By interpreting the situation differently, I cheered myself up and achieved a higher score on the next test. To conclude, I believe that being positive is essential for people. Even in depressing situations, optimistic people can easily improve their mood and not waste too much time worrying. Therefore, I have to say that being positive is one of the most important aspects of life.

Tip

1. This question is similar to Question Type 7, but you are given an additional 30 seconds to prepare.
2. There is no minimum or maximum word limit, but write enough so that you can demonstrate your thoughts and writing skills.
3. Use a variety of sentence structures and word choices.
4. Write a logical response with supporting details.
5. Take the last minute to proofread your writing.

2

0:30

Prepare to write about the topic below.

You will have 5 minutes to write.

Describe the last time you were emotionally moved by a TV show or movie. Why did you find it so moving, and how did it make you feel?

NEXT

5:00

Write about the topic below for 5 minutes.

Describe the last time you were emotionally moved by a TV show or movie. Why did you find it so moving, and how did it make you feel?

Your response

YOU CAN CONTINUE AFTER 3 MINUTES

I recently watched the film *Dune* in a movie theater, and I found both its story and its visuals to be emotionally moving. For one thing, the story was epic and immersive. It was easy to get swept up by the scope of the sci-fi drama and action, especially since the actors did such a fantastic job portraying the characters. I was so worried for the main character as he endured hardship after hardship, even though I knew he was not a real person. In addition, the visuals were breathtaking. Every scene was beautiful, whether it was a majestic shot of a desert sunset or a dreadful glimpse of a massive enemy army. Without a doubt, the theater, with its high-resolution screen and cutting-edge audio system, helped make the movie feel larger than life. All of these qualities came together to make *Dune* an overwhelming cinematic experience, and by the end of the film, I had felt every emotion imaginable.

Speaking Sample

I. All About the Question Type

Key Points

- Read a written prompt and speak a response that demonstrates your speaking skills
- Your Speaking Sample will be available to the universities that receive your results
- Preparation time: 30 seconds
- Duration: You need to write for a minimum of 1 minute and a maximum of 3 minutes
- Only 1 question of this question type appears usually as the 36th question

Which Subscores are Assessed

- Conversation: Ability to listen and speak
- Production: Ability to write and speak

How the Question is Presented

① A screen that directs you to make sure you are centered in the camera frame will appear for 30 seconds.

0:30

Speaking Sample

Make sure you are centered in the camera frame for the speaking sample.

NEXT

---

② The question will appear on the screen when the 30-second timer begins.

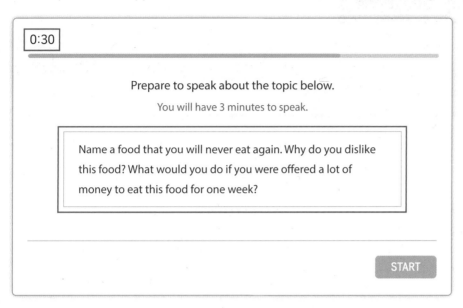

③ Speak your response for a minimum of 1 minute and a maximum of 3 minutes, then submit your response.

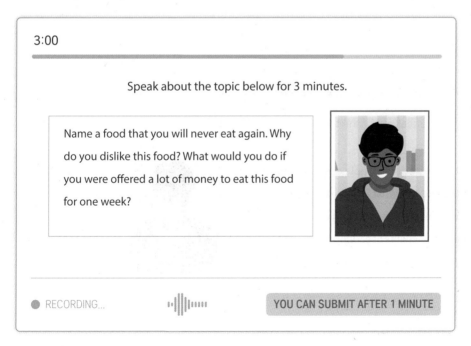

II. Exercise Questions

1

0:30

Prepare to speak about the topic below.

You will have 3 minutes to speak.

> Describe one way that people can make money using the
> Internet. What are some ways that you have thought about
> making money online? What are the benefits of earning income
> through the Internet?

START

3:00

Speak about the topic below for 3 minutes.

> Describe one way that people can make money
> using the Internet. What are some ways that
> you have thought about making money online?
> What are the benefits of earning income
> through the Internet?

● RECORDING...   YOU CAN SUBMIT AFTER 1 MINUTE

One effective way to make money through the Internet is by providing services on online platforms. These days, there are a variety of websites people can utilize to provide a service. For instance, a teacher can offer online English classes to their students through a social media website. In my case, I have thought about making money online by running a YouTube channel or selling products on my Instagram account. In fact, I have made some profit by selling clothes I bought in Korea to people overseas. It was incredibly simple since we could just communicate through social media without having to meet in person.

The major benefit of earning income through the Internet is that I can work anytime, anywhere. For example, if I were to run a YouTube channel, I could shoot videos in my free time and upload them from any place that has access to the Internet. Therefore, I think earning income through the Internet has many benefits for people in modern society.

Tip

1. Remember that universities can view a video recording of your response, so mind your facial expressions and speak confidently.
2. Since this question is similar to Question Type 8 and Question Type 9, use the same speaking strategies to form your answer.
3. Include personal experiences in your examples.
4. Speak for 1 to 3 minutes, then click SUBMIT to conclude your test.

0:30

Prepare to speak about the topic below.

You will have 3 minutes to speak.

Do you think we should always forgive others, regardless of how poorly they have behaved? Explain your reasoning.

START

3:00

Speak about the topic below for 3 minutes.

Do you think we should always forgive others, regardless of how poorly they have behaved? Explain your reasoning.

● RECORDING...   YOU CAN SUBMIT AFTER 1 MINUTE

No matter how poorly a person has acted, it is always best for us to choose forgiveness, because it allows the relationship to heal and improve. Most of all, we can never know the full story behind why someone behaves poorly. Maybe the person was having a particularly difficult day or dealing with some terrible news. There's always some sort of motivation behind a person's negative actions, but we rarely know what it is. We can, however, prevent ourselves from judging them too harshly and decide to forgive them.

In addition, forgiveness will give the relationship a chance to heal. Without forgiveness, one negative action results in another, and this causes an endless cycle of negativity. The relationship will only worsen until there is no chance of saving it. However, if one person can decide to forgive the other, then the negative cycle ends. The relationship can return to normal or even become stronger than before. Therefore, forgiveness will always lead to better results.

Chapter

2

DET Practice Test

duolingo english test

Practice Test

1

1:00

Select the real English words in this list.

station	tinford	statech	bowl	physics	surganize
thanss	warddes	champagne	crisided	niking	teenager
himil	luckle	healthy	mecon	trodul	racess

NEXT

2

3:00

Type the missing letters to complete the text below.

My Favorite Musical Number

Following a long interlude, the main melody returns at a slower tempo.

After q u o ____ the q u e s ____ "w h ____?"
from t ____ opening, the s o ____ closes w i ____ a
"ghostly b r e ____" f i n ____ answering t ____
question: "T h ____ where y ____ are n ____ , t h ____ is
h a p p ____ ." The song concludes in its original key.

NEXT

3

1:00

Type the statement that you hear.

Your response

Number of replays left: 2

NEXT

AT-03

4

1:00

Write a description of the image below for 1 minute.

Your response

NEXT

5

1:00

Write a description of the image below for 1 minute.

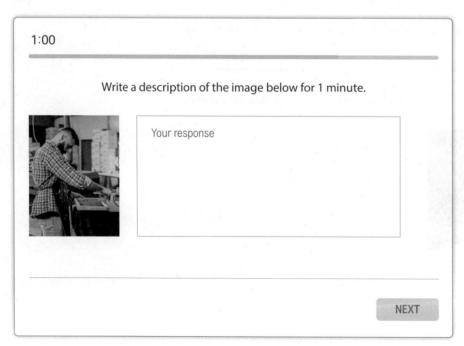

Your response

NEXT

6

1:00

Write a description of the image below for 1 minute.

Your response

NEXT

7

0:20

Record yourself saying the statement below.

"People make new things, and conversely, many scientific endeavors are possible through technologies."

RECORD NOW

8

1:00

Type the statement that you hear.

Your response

Number of replays left: 2

NEXT

9

0:20

Record yourself saying the statement below.

"The ballet overall stays generally lighthearted for its running time of an hour and forty minutes."

RECORD NOW

10

1:00

Type the statement that you hear.

Your response

Number of replays left: 2

NEXT

AT-10

11

Record yourself saying the statement below.

"There's hardly any hope that he'll win the election."

RECORD NOW

12

3:00

Type the missing letters to complete the text below.

Aristotle Onassis, the Shipping Tycoon

He decided to invest in shipping and eventually owned an impressive fleet of cargo ships, making him one of the richest men in the world. In 1957, h founded Olympic Airways. He c o n v one o his s h into a luxury y a called Christina, w h he u s to e n t e famous p e o (a r t , p o l i t , r o y e .).

NEXT

13

1:00

Select the real English words in this list.

qualitical	occamps	humanity	hostile	gadget	domain
vertical	medication	refusal	scarce	dominance	costrict
philoso	dominate	redevelopment	flick	compensate	resumedialed

NEXT

14

0:20

Record yourself saying the statement below.

"After a team captures all four territories, that team must capture the enemy team's base."

RECORD NOW

15

1:00

Type the statement that you hear.

Your response

Number of replays left: 2

NEXT

AT-15

16

1:00

Select the real English words in this list.

outbreak | materialist | respensent | clarity | concession | symbat

immational | refined | unaffected | incormation | squeel | yolegent

wreck | meticulous | contemplate | tritulard | knowingly | eminent

NEXT

17

3:00

Type the missing letters to complete the text below.

Consumer Spending on the Rise

More than half of the population depends on agriculture. Industrial

a ☐ service s e c ☐ are g r o ☐ in

i m p o r ☐ and a c c ☐ for 25% a ☐

51% of GDP, r e s p e c ☐ , w h ☐ agriculture

c o n t r ☐ about 25.6% o ☐ GDP. While a quarter of

the population is impoverished, a growing middle class possesses disposable

income for consumer goods.

NEXT

18

1:00

Type the statement that you hear.

Your response

Number of replays left: 2

NEXT

19

0:20

Record yourself saying the statement below.

"It can be considered as the moral or the sole truth of the universe."

RECORD NOW

20

1:00

Type the statement that you hear.

Your response

Number of replays left: 2

NEXT

AT-20

1:00

Select the real English words in this list.

erode	fragrant	breadth	entibality	prospersible	hazardous
intriguing	tendurand	intrusion	nostalgia	ventablent	undelending
shattered	unethical	conciness	flawless	adjacent	fragrance

NEXT

0:20

Record yourself saying the statement below.

"He looked at the people who looked at the pictures, instead of at the pictures themselves."

RECORD NOW

3:00

Type the missing letters to complete the text below.

The Rise of Cities

Early advancements in modern civilizations were a result of developments in agriculture. A sta___ and reli___ source o__ crops all l_____ populations t__ stay i__ one reg____. In mo__ recent ti_____, ferti_____ significantly incr_____ the to____ harvest poss_____. Greater production meant larger populations could be supported.

NEXT

0:30

Interactive reading

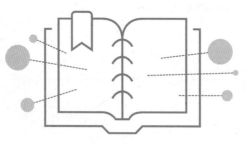

You will have 8 minutes to answer questions about a reading passage.

NEXT

8:00   for the next 6 questions

QUIT TEST

PASSAGE

In order to ① stop / increase / find/ keep / be your air conditioner operating in peak condition, it should ② see / place / set / receive / find regular maintenance. A simple maintenance plan will be able to ③ maintain / catch / function / put / lease any issues with your unit ④ upon / to / so / before / until they can become ⑤ now / serious / unsure / earlier / like problems. You'll ⑥ show / take / put / end up spending much more money ⑦ maybe / now / if / then you fix problems after they occur compared to paying ⑧ to / for / with / sure / when a maintenance plan, so it is prudent to be proactive with air conditioner care.

Select the best option for each missing word.

① Select a word	∨
② Select a word	∨
③ Select a word	∨
④ Select a word	∨
⑤ Select a word	∨
⑥ Select a word	∨
⑦ Select a word	∨
⑧ Select a word	∨

NEXT

3:49   for the next 5 questions

QUIT TEST

PASSAGE

In order to keep your air conditioner operating in peak condition, it should receive regular maintenance. A simple maintenance plan will be able to catch any issues with your unit before they can become serious problems. You'll end up spending much more money if you fix problems after they occur compared to paying for a maintenance plan, so it is prudent to be proactive with air conditioner care.

Replacing or repairing a broken air conditioner also takes a long time, during which you'll have to rely on a small and inefficient window unit.

Select the best sentence to fill in the blank in the passage.

○ They offer after-service care that helps keep their customers' air conditioning units up to date.

○ It will save you time and money while adding years to your unit's life cycle.

○ If you are unable to make the repairs yourself, call a professional before causing further damage.

○ With temperatures at record highs, the guys knew that they needed to get a new air conditioner to beat the heat.

NEXT

3:09   for the next 4 questions

QUIT TEST

PASSAGE

In order to keep your air conditioner operating in peak condition, it should receive regular maintenance. A simple maintenance plan will be able to catch any issues with your unit before they can become serious problems. You'll end up spending much more money if you fix problems after they occur compared to paying for a maintenance plan, so it is prudent to be proactive with air conditioner care. It will save you time and money while adding years to your unit's life cycle. Replacing or repairing a broken air conditioner also takes a long time, during which you'll have to rely on a small and inefficient window unit.

Click and drag text to highlight the answer to the question below.

What happens if you don't pay for regular maintenance?

Highlight text in the passage to set an answer

NEXT

2:17   for the next 3 questions   QUIT TEST

PASSAGE

In order to keep your air conditioner operating in peak condition, it should receive regular maintenance. A simple maintenance plan will be able to catch any issues with your unit before they can become serious problems. You'll end up spending much more money if you fix problems after they occur compared to paying for a maintenance plan, so it is prudent to be proactive with air conditioner care. It will save you time and money while adding years to your unit's life cycle. Replacing or repairing a broken air conditioner also takes a long time, during which you'll have to rely on a small and inefficient window unit.

Click and drag text to highlight the answer to the question below.

What will you have to use if your air conditioner breaks?

Highlight text in the passage to set an answer

NEXT

QUIT TEST

PASSAGE

In order to keep your air conditioner operating in peak condition, it should receive regular maintenance. A simple maintenance plan will be able to catch any issues with your unit before they can become serious problems. You'll end up spending much more money if you fix problems after they occur compared to paying for a maintenance plan, so it is prudent to be proactive with air conditioner care. It will save you time and money while adding years to your unit's life cycle. Replacing or repairing a broken air conditioner also takes a long time, during which you'll have to rely on a small and inefficient window unit.

Select the idea that is expressed in the passage.

○ A company may not pay for the proper care of the air conditioner because it is too expensive.

○ Central air conditioning has the advantage of keeping a consistent temperature throughout the house.

○ Regular maintenance will keep your air conditioner working well as it will prevent major problems from occurring.

○ Maintenance teams are responsible for installing customer air conditioners and repairing units that are under warranty.

NEXT

1:03   for this question   QUIT TEST

PASSAGE

In order to keep your air conditioner operating in peak condition, it should receive regular maintenance. A simple maintenance plan will be able to catch any issues with your unit before they can become serious problems. You'll end up spending much more money if you fix problems after they occur compared to paying for a maintenance plan, so it is prudent to be proactive with air conditioner care. It will save you time and money while adding years to your unit's life cycle. Replacing or repairing a broken air conditioner also takes a long time, during which you'll have to rely on a small and inefficient window unit.

Select the best title for the passage.

○ Taking Care of Your Air Conditioner

○ Advances in Air Conditioning

○ Proper Fridge Maintenance

○ Ideal Home Temperatures

NEXT

0:30

Interactive reading

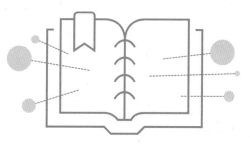

You will have 7 minutes to answer questions about a reading passage.

NEXT

7:00   for the next 6 questions   QUIT TEST

PASSAGE

Public health nurses are ① like / part / inside / considered / piece of a long tradition in the United States. The first public health ② team / nurses / couple / group / members in the country appeared in 1854 in Boston. They worked ③ as / other / while / from / at visiting nurses in a smallpox emergency room. They treated diseased patients and informed families about smallpox prevention. Realizing the effectiveness of public health services in treating smallpox epidemics, the Massachusetts Board of State Charities ④ gathered / made / comes / of / brought together nurses and state health ⑤ students / institutions / doctors / personnel / officials .

Select the best option for each missing word.

① Select a word	∨
② Select a word	∨
③ Select a word	∨
④ Select a word	∨
⑤ Select a word	∨

NEXT

PASSAGE

Public health nurses are part of a long tradition in the United States. The first public health nurses in the country appeared in 1854 in Boston. They worked as visiting nurses in a smallpox emergency room. They treated diseased patients and informed families about smallpox prevention. Realizing the effectiveness of public health services in treating smallpox epidemics, the Massachusetts Board of State Charities brought together nurses and state health officials.

_____

_____

She was an early advocate of public health rights.

Select the best sentence to fill in the blank in the passage.

- ○ As healthcare expanded from local doctors on house calls to hospitals as medical centers, the need for nurses grew.

- ○ Local clinics were small and located in residential neighborhoods to serve patients who lived and worked nearby.

- ○ The work of Lillian Wald, who founded the Henry Street Settlement in New York City, helped establish public health nursing.

- ○ It provides the means for patients to receive the care and attention they need to live healthier, longer lives.

NEXT

3:16   for the next 4 questions   QUIT TEST

PASSAGE

Public health nurses are part of a long tradition in the United States. The first public health nurses in the country appeared in 1854 in Boston. They worked as visiting nurses in a smallpox emergency room. They treated diseased patients and informed families about smallpox prevention. Realizing the effectiveness of public health services in treating smallpox epidemics, the Massachusetts Board of State Charities brought together nurses and state health officials. The work of Lillian Wald, who founded the Henry Street Settlement in New York City, helped establish public health nursing. She was an early advocate of public health rights.

Click and drag text to highlight the answer to the question below.

What responsibilities did public health nurses have in Boston in 1854?

Highlight text in the passage to set an answer

NEXT

QUIT TEST

PASSAGE

Public health nurses are part of a long tradition in the United States. The first public health nurses in the country appeared in 1854 in Boston. They worked as visiting nurses in a smallpox emergency room. They treated diseased patients and informed families about smallpox prevention. Realizing the effectiveness of public health services in treating smallpox epidemics, the Massachusetts Board of State Charities brought together nurses and state health officials. The work of Lillian Wald, who founded the Henry Street Settlement in New York City, helped establish public health nursing. She was an early advocate of public health rights.

Click and drag text to highlight the answer to the question below.

What did the Massachusetts Board of State Charities do?

Highlight text in the passage to set an answer

NEXT

1:47   for the next 2 questions

QUIT TEST

PASSAGE

Public health nurses are part of a long tradition in the United States. The first public health nurses in the country appeared in 1854 in Boston. They worked as visiting nurses in a smallpox emergency room. They treated diseased patients and informed families about smallpox prevention. Realizing the effectiveness of public health services in treating smallpox epidemics, the Massachusetts Board of State Charities brought together nurses and state health officials. The work of Lillian Wald, who founded the Henry Street Settlement in New York City, helped establish public health nursing. She was an early advocate of public health rights.

Select the idea that is expressed in the passage.

○ Public health nursing started in the United States during a smallpox epidemic in Boston in 1854.

○ Physician's assistants were one of the first professional healthcare positions and were in high demand in the late 1800s.

○ As new advances in medicine were developed, the field of nursing grew.

○ Public health nurses helped make healthcare more accessible to all people, no matter their class or race.

NEXT

1:00   for this question   QUIT TEST

PASSAGE

Public health nurses are part of a long tradition in the United States. The first public health nurses in the country appeared in 1854 in Boston. They worked as visiting nurses in a smallpox emergency room. They treated diseased patients and informed families about smallpox prevention. Realizing the effectiveness of public health services in treating smallpox epidemics, the Massachusetts Board of State Charities brought together nurses and state health officials. The work of Lillian Wald, who founded the Henry Street Settlement in New York City, helped establish public health nursing. She was an early advocate of public health rights.

Select the best title for the passage.

○ Medical Technology in the 19th Century

○ Social Responsibility in Healthcare

○ Smallpox in the United States

○ The Origins of Public Health Nursing

NEXT

0:30

Interactive reading

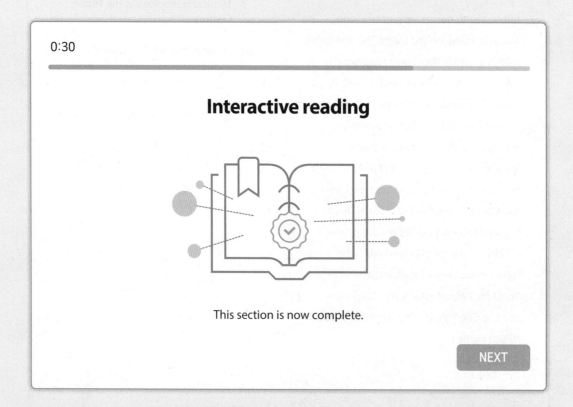

This section is now complete.

NEXT

for the next 5 questions

QUIT TEST

You will participate in a conversation about the scenario below.

You are a student in a business studies class. After today's lecture on business management, you approach your professor to ask them more about the concept of team role theory.

START

3:30 for the next 5 questions

QUIT TEST

Question 1 of 5

Pick the best option to start the conversation.

○ Excuse me, Professor. I have some questions about the exam we just took.

○ Hi, Professor. Would you mind reviewing the first draft of my essay?

○ Professor Atkins, I'm afraid I was unable to attend the lecture earlier today.

○ Do you have a moment, Professor Atkins? I'd like your opinion on a book I am reading.

○ Hi, Professor. I had a question about something you mentioned in today's lecture.

NEXT

3:00   for the next 4 questions   QUIT TEST

Hi, Professor. I had a question about something you mentioned in today's lecture.

Listen closely! You can only play the audio clips once.

AT-26-01

Question 2 of 5

Select the best response.

○ Thanks for your explanation. I understand it a lot better now.

○ That's right. I'm struggling to understand how it is applied in a business setting.

○ I found all the lectures really informative and beneficial.

○ Exactly! That's the same conclusion that I came to about the lecture.

○ I'm hoping that you plan to include team role theory in one of our upcoming lectures.

NEXT

 No problem. I'm always happy to help my students. You must be talking about my lecture on team role theory.

That's right. I'm struggling to understand how it is applied in a business setting.

◁)) AT-26-02

Question 3 of 5

Select the best response.

○ I think that's true for many different types of jobs at the moment.

○ That's a great tip. Hopefully, after I listen to her talk, I'll understand things more.

○ Well, I guess I would be able to do that for you if it would be helpful to my classmates.

○ I think one would be a leader and another one must be a good communicator.

○ I'm afraid I haven't had a lot of experience when it comes to being a group leader.

NEXT

2:00 for the next 2 questions

QUIT TEST

 Well, that's a good question. According to Dr. Meredith Belbin's Team Role Theory, each of us is suited to a particular role within a team, and there are 9 types of roles. Can you guess what any of those are?

I think one would be a leader and another one must be a good communicator.

🔊 AT-26-03

Question 4 of 5

Select the best response.

- ○ You're right. I'm more comfortable working on my own rather than in a team.

- ○ I get it! That's a great way to find a role that suits each member of a team.

- ○ That probably is my greatest weakness. I'll just need to keep studying hard.

- ○ Well, if you think it would be helpful, I'd be happy to take on a different role.

- ○ I had no idea that marketing was so important to businesses these days.

NEXT

1:30 for this question

QUIT TEST

 That's right. And a team needs an ideas person, and someone who can support others, and an expert, or specialist, in a subject. The theory is important in business, as it helps us identify roles that are not suited to an individual rather than just considering these as weaknesses.

I get it! That's a great way to find a role that suits each member of a team.

🔊 AT-26-04

Question 5 of 5

Select the best response.

○ Great idea! I'll purchase a ticket as soon as I get home.

○ I'll definitely read more textbooks before the exam comes.

○ Thanks for the recommendation. I'll be sure to check it out.

○ Oh, I didn't realize I could visit that place in person.

○ Yes, meeting Dr. Belbin really helped me to understand the theory better.

NEXT

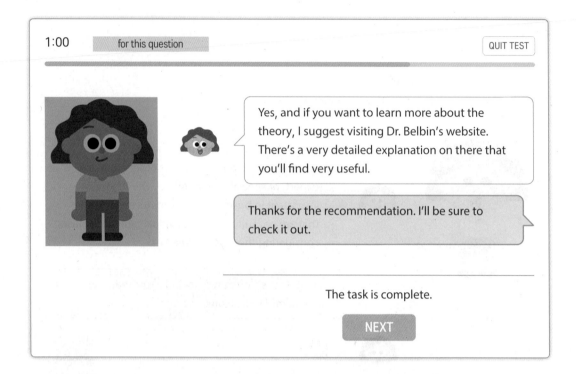

Yes, and if you want to learn more about the theory, I suggest visiting Dr. Belbin's website. There's a very detailed explanation on there that you'll find very useful.

Thanks for the recommendation. I'll be sure to check it out.

The task is complete.

NEXT

26-6

1:15 QUIT TEST

Summarize the conversation you just had in 75 seconds.

Your response

NEXT

4:00   for the next 5 questions   QUIT TEST

You will participate in a conversation about the scenario below.

You are thinking about moving out of the university's halls of residence next year and are discussing it with your friend.

START

3:30   for the next 5 questions   QUIT TEST

Listen closely! You can only play the audio clips once.

AT-27-01

Question 1 of 5
Select the best response.

○ I'm pleased to hear that you are doing the same as me.

○ Oh, really? Which building do you currently stay in?

○ I'd like to find out more information about the halls of residence.

○ Actually, I was considering moving into an apartment instead.

○ I think around 500 students live there at the moment.

NEXT

3:00   for the next 4 questions   QUIT TEST

So, are you going to continue living in the halls of residence next year?

Actually, I was considering moving into an apartment instead.

▶

AT-27-02

Question 2 of 5

Select the best response.

- ○ My landlord has recently agreed to lower my rent by $50 per month.

- ○ I cannot believe you pay so much! Have you thought about moving out?

- ○ Yes, and it's located in such a convenient location near the university.

- ○ Perhaps you could work part-time to boost your monthly income.

- ○ I did think about that, but I'll be able to afford it with my part-time job.

NEXT

 Are you sure that's a good idea? Rent for apartments is so high these days.

I did think about that, but I'll be able to afford it with my part-time job.

  ▶

AT-27-03

Question 3 of 5

Select the best response.

○ Sure! I'd love to live with you. Let's take a look at some apartments this weekend.

○ I'm not too bothered about that. I have a pass that gets me 50 percent off all journeys.

○ You're right. I suppose there are other universities that might offer the same advantages.

○ Well, if you'd prefer to go by car, I could pick you up and we could get to the event faster.

○ That's a good point. The halls of residence are located a great distance from the university.

NEXT

2:00　for the next 2 questions　　　　　QUIT TEST

 I guess so, but the halls of residence are so cheap and conveniently located. If you live in your own apartment, you'll need to take the bus to the university.

I'm not too bothered about that. I have a pass that gets me 50 percent off all journeys.

AT-27-04

Question 4 of 5

Select the best response.

○ It might take some getting used to, but living by myself will provide me with a nice, quiet study environment.

○ I think you'll find that you'll make a lot of new friends once you start attending university.

○ We've known each other for almost four years and we still hang out whenever we get a chance.

○ That could work, but we'll need to split the rent payments and all the monthly utility bills.

○ In that case, I'd better check what the monthly rate is in that particular neighborhood.

NEXT

1:30   for this question   QUIT TEST

 That's pretty good, but won't you miss all your university friends if you live alone rather than in the halls of residence?

It might take some getting used to, but living by myself will provide me with a nice, quiet study environment.

🔊 AT-27-05

Question 5 of 5

Select the best response.

- ○ That's a shame! I thought you really enjoyed attending those classes.

- ○ Once I decide on the specific date, I'll let you know so you can add it to your calendar.

- ○ I appreciate your concern. I'll definitely think more about it and weigh up the pros and cons.

- ○ I'm glad that you didn't run into it. It's a really important decision to make.

- ○ Well, if you need any tips about finding an apartment, feel free to ask me.

NEXT

I suppose I can see some benefits now that you've explained them. I just think you should give it some thought before making a final decision.

I appreciate your concern. I'll definitely think more about it and weigh up the pros and cons.

The task is complete.

NEXT

27-6

Summarize the conversation you just had in 75 seconds.

Your response

NEXT

0:30

Prepare to write about the topic below.

You will have 5 minutes to write.

When choosing a career, the most important thing to consider is the salary (how much money you will earn). Do you agree or disagree? Give specific reasons for your answer.

START

5:00

Write about the topic below for 5 minutes.

When choosing a career, the most important thing to consider is the salary (how much money you will earn). Do you agree or disagree? Give specific reasons for your answer.

Your response

YOU CAN CONTINUE AFTER 3 MINUTES

0:20

Prepare to speak about the topic below.

You will have 90 seconds to speak.

Number of replays left: 2

RECORD NOW

◁◁)) AT-29

1:30

Speak about the topic for 90 seconds.

Number of replays left: 0

● RECORDING...

YOU CAN CONTINUE AFTER 30 SECONDS

0:20

Prepare to speak about the image below.

You will have 90 seconds to speak.

RECORD NOW

1:30

Speak about the image below for 90 seconds.

● RECORDING...   YOU CAN CONTINUE AFTER 30 SECONDS

0:20

Prepare to speak about the topic below.

You will have 90 seconds to speak.

Discuss how people commute to work.

• How do people commute to work?

• How long do people spend commuting?

• How will commuting change in the future?

RECORD NOW

1:30

Speak about the topic below for 90 seconds.

Discuss how people commute to work.

• How do people commute to work?

• How long do people spend commuting?

• How will commuting change in the future?

 RECORDING...   YOU CAN CONTINUE AFTER 30 SECONDS

32

 AT-32

0:20

Prepare to speak about the topic below.

You will have 90 seconds to speak.

Number of replays left: 2

RECORD NOW

1:30

Speak about the topic for 90 seconds.

Number of replays left: 0

● RECORDING... 　　　　YOU CAN CONTINUE AFTER 30 SECONDS

0:30

Writing & Speaking Sample

The next 2 questions will contribute to your score and will also be available to the institutions that receive your results.

NEXT

0:30

Prepare to write about the topic below.

You will have 5 minutes to write.

> Many people feel that it is important to learn history in order
> to understand the past. Do you agree or disagree with this
> statement? Support your opinion with examples from your
> personal experiences and observations.

START

5:00

Write about the topic below for 5 minutes.

Many people feel that it is important
to learn history in order to understand
the past. Do you agree or disagree with
this statement? Support your opinion
with examples from your personal
experiences and observations.

Your response

YOU CAN CONTINUE AFTER 3 MINUTES

0:30

Speaking Sample

Make sure you are centered in the camera frame for the speaking sample.

NEXT

0:30

Prepare to speak about the topic below.

You will have 3 minutes to speak.

> Name something you do when you are feeling creative. How does this activity open your imagination? What can your friends learn from you to improve their creativity?

START

3:00

Speak about the topic below for 3 minutes.

> Name something you do when you are feeling creative. How does this activity open your imagination? What can your friends learn from you to improve their creativity?

● RECORDING...   YOU CAN SUBMIT AFTER 1 MINUTE

1

station, bowl, physics, champagne, teenager, healthy

2

Following a long interlude, the main melody returns at a slower tempo. After quoting the question "where?" from the opening, the song closes with a "ghostly breath" finally answering the question: "There where you are not, there is happiness." The song concludes in its original key.

3

I'll go talk to them right now.

4

This is a photograph of a firefighter spraying a car with water from a hose. In detail, he is wearing a helmet and a yellow and black jacket. It looks like there is some smoke around the car, so maybe there was a fire. The water looks very powerful.

5

This is a photograph of two men sitting at a table and looking at a laptop computer. In detail, the man on the left is wearing a blue shirt, and the man on the right is wearing a white shirt. They are smiling and laughing, so maybe they are watching a funny video.

6

This is a photograph of a man working in a machine shop. In detail, he is standing at a machine, but I am not sure what it does. He is wearing a blue flannel shirt, blue jeans, and an apron with paint splattered on it. He seems to be concentrating on his work.

7

People make new things, and conversely, many scientific endeavors are possible through technologies.

8

I had already gone to bed when the telephone rang.

9

The ballet overall stays generally lighthearted for its running time of an hour and forty minutes.

10

If you had a million yen, what would you do with it?

11

There's hardly any hope that he'll win the election.

12

He decided to invest in shipping and eventually owned an impressive fleet of cargo ships, making him one of the richest men in the world. In 1957, he founded Olympic Airways. He converted one of his ships into a luxury yacht called Christina, which he used to entertain famous people (artists, politicians, royalty, etc.).

13

humanity, hostile, gadget, domain, vertical, medication, refusal, scarce, dominance, dominate, redevelopment, flick, compensate

14

After a team captures all four territories, that team must capture the enemy team's base.

15

The human voice is produced by the larynx.

16

outbreak, materialist, clarity, refined, unaffected, wreck, meticulous, contemplate, knowingly, eminent

17

More than half of the population depends on agriculture. Industrial and service sectors are growing in importance and account for 25% and 51% of GDP, respectively, while agriculture contributes about 25.6% of GDP. While a quarter of the population is impoverished, a growing middle class possesses disposable income for consumer goods.

18

There are more than one hundred species of mammals here.

Practice Test Answers

19

It can be considered as the moral or the sole truth of the universe.

20

The study of metal alloys is a large part of material science.

21

erode, fragrant, breadth, hazardous, intriguing, intrusion, nostalgia, shattered, unethical, flawless, adjacent, fragrance

22

He looked at the people who looked at the pictures, instead of at the pictures themselves.

23

Early advancements in modern civilizations were a result of developments in agriculture. A stable and reliable source of crops allowed populations to stay in one region. In more recent times, fertilizing significantly increased the total harvest possible. Greater production meant larger populations could be supported.

Interactive Reading

24-1

① keep ② receive ③ catch ④ before ⑤ serious ⑥ end ⑦ if ⑧ for

24-2

(2) It will save you time and money while adding years to your unit's life cycle.

24-3

You'll end up spending much more money if you fix problems after they occur compared to paying for a maintenance plan

24-4

you'll have to rely on a small and inefficient window unit.

(3) Regular maintenance will keep your air conditioner working well as it will prevent major problems from occurring.

24-6

(1) Taking Care of Your Air Conditioner

Interactive Reading

25-1

① part ② nurses ③ as ④ brought ⑤ officials

25-2

(3) The work of Lillian Wald, who founded the Henry Street Settlement in New York City, helped establish public health nursing.

25-3

They treated diseased patients and informed families about smallpox prevention.

25-4

the Massachusetts Board of State Charities brought together nurses and state health officials.

25-5

(1) Public health nursing started in the United States during a smallpox epidemic in Boston in 1854.

25-6

(4) The Origins of Public Health Nursing

Interactive Listening

26-1

(5) Hi, Professor. I had a question about something you mentioned in today's lecture.

26-2

(2) That's right. I'm struggling to understand how it is applied in a business setting.

26-3

(4) I think one would be a leader and another one must be a good communicator.

26-4

(2) I get it! That's a great way to find a role that suits each member of a team.

26-5

(3) Thanks for the recommendation. I'll be sure to check it out.

26-6

I was speaking to my professor because I had difficulty understanding her lecture on team role theory. She explained the basics of the theory and gave me some examples, which helped me to understand. In the end, she advised me to check out a website for more detailed information.

Interactive Listening

27-1

(4) Actually, I was considering moving into an apartment instead.

27-2

(5) I did think about that, but I'll be able to afford it with my part-time job.

27-3

(2) I'm not too bothered about that. I have a pass that gets me 50 percent off all journeys.

27-4

(1) It might take some getting used to, but living by myself will provide me with a nice, quiet study environment.

27-5

(3) I appreciate your concern. I'll definitely think more about it and weigh up the pros and cons.

27-6

I was speaking with my friend about how I was thinking about moving out of the halls of residence and into an apartment. He thought it was a bad idea because it is cheaper and more convenient to stay in the halls. I explained that I could afford it and how it could help me study. In the end, I agreed that I should give the issue more thought.

28

Some people believe that the salary, or how much money they will make, is the most important factor when choosing a career, but I do not agree with them. While the money you will make must be considered, it should not take top priority. For one thing, you need to make sure that you can excel in the career. For example, surgeons make a lot of money, but I know that I could never do what they do. In addition, since it is your career, it will be a major part of your life. Therefore, you should at least have some passion for what you are doing. If you do not like what you do, then you will struggle to do it every day.

29

In what ways can a person be supportive of a friend or relative who's going through a difficult time?

There are several ways a person can be supportive of a friend or family member who's going through a difficult time. Most importantly, they should listen. A lot of people have a hard time talking about their personal problems, so if they feel comfortable with you, then they'll be able to talk to you. Second, you can try to get their mind off the problem. Sometimes, people don't want to focus on the problem. Instead, you could take them out to do something fun. It might distract them from their worries for a little bit. If it's a problem they can't really solve, then this is the best thing for them.

30

This is a picture of a man pulling a boat ashore. In detail, I can see that he is wearing a tan jacket and pants. On top of that, he is crouching down and using both hands to pull on the rope. From this, I can infer that the boat is heavy. Therefore, it is obvious that the man must be having a hard time pulling the boat by himself. And, in the background, there are some tall trees and calm water. This clearly shows that the man is by a river.

31

Most people commute to work by using public transportation or by driving themselves. The subway in my city is very efficient, so most people can use it to get to their workplace. The average commuting time is probably around 45 minutes to an hour, somewhere around there. I think public transportation will be improved in the future. It will be more efficient and use cleaner energy. Or, maybe more people will work from home, so they won't even need to commute.

32

What arrangements do you need to make before you take a trip?

Before a trip, I need to make several arrangements, like my travel reservations. I'll book a ticket online or with an app. Once I know the travel dates, then I can start looking for a place to stay during my trip. I usually stay in hotels, so I compare all the prices in the area. After that, I just need to request the time off from work, and then the day before the trip, I'll pack my bags. Oh, there's one more thing. I need to drop my dog off at my friend's house, too.

33

I agree with the statement that it is important to learn history in order to understand the past for several reasons.

First of all, by studying the past, we can identify historical trends. These show how past civilizations and societies have handled major events like wars, economic growth and decline, and social change. For example, people still study ancient Rome to better understand why the empire collapsed. By doing so, historians and political scientists can highlight similarities between the past and present, and hopefully prevent a similar outcome for our current society.

In addition, we can better understand how society has changed and progressed. Sometimes, we feel like everything is worse nowadays, but by studying history, you can see how much we have improved. Through technology and social change, we have come a long way in making society better. It is important to see how this has been done so that we can continue making improvements in the future.

In these ways, studying history helps us to continue moving forward instead of backward.

34

I don't feel like I'm the most creative person, but I have started sketching and drawing on my iPad. It's kind of a new hobby of mine. Sometimes, when I want to relax and just let my mind wander, I'll start drawing on my iPad. It's really easy to do, and by following a YouTube video or tutorial, I can create some really neat drawings. It makes me feel like I'm much better at drawing than I actually am, but that's okay. I've started sketching more of my own illustrations because it's helped me become more creative. I even have some ideas for a few comics, but I'm not ready for that yet.

I guess if my friends can learn anything from me, it's that you don't need to be great at it to be creative. Just do it, you know? It's about how you feel when you're being creative, not what you're actually making. Maybe it's a sort of therapy. It really is a great way to deal with stress, so I think everyone should try to add some creativity to their lives.

Memo

Appendix

DET Vocabulary

☐ **abroad**
adv. [əbrɔ́ːd]

= overseas

☐ **abrupt**
adj. [əbrʌ́pt]

n. abruptness
adv. abruptly

☐ **academic**
adj. [ækədémik]

n. academy, academia
adv. academically

☐ **acceptable**
adj. [ækséptəbl]
adj. [əkséptəbl]

n. acceptance
v. accept, accepted, accepting
adv. acceptably

☐ **accommodate**
v. [əkámədeit]

n. accommodation
v. accommodated, accommodating
adj. accommodative

☐ **accountable**
adj. [əkáuntəbl]

n. accountability
v. account, accounted, accounting

☐ **achieve**
v. [ətʃíːv]

n. achievement, achiever
v. achieved, achieving
adj. achievable

☐ **acidic**
adj. [əsídik]

n. acid, acidity
adj. acid

☐ **acknowledgement**
n. [æknálidʒmənt]

v. acknowledge, acknowledged, acknowledging

☐ **acoustic**
adj. [əkúːstik]

adv. acoustically

☐ **across**
adv. prep. [əkrɔ́ːs]

= transverse

☐ **adaptable**
adj. [ədǽptəbl]

n. adaptability, adaptation
v. adapt, adapted, adapting
adj. adaptive

☐ **add**
v. [æd]

n. addition
v. added, adding
adj. additional

☐ **addictive**
adj. [ədíktiv]

n. addiction
v. addict, addicted, addicting

☐ **address**
n. [ǽdres]
v. [ədrés]

n. addressee
v. addressed, addressing

☐ **adjustable**
adj. [ədʒʌ́stəbl]

n. adjustability, adjustment
v. adjust, adjusted, adjusting

☐ **administer**
v. [ədmínistər]

n. administration, administrator
v. administered, administering
adj. administrative

☐ **administration**
n. [ədmìnistréiʃən]

n. administrator
v. administer, administered, administering
adj. administrative

☐ **admire**
v. [ədmáiər]

n. admirer
v. admired, admiring
adj. admiring
adv. admiringly

☐ **adopt**
v. [ədápt]

n. adoption, adopter
v. adopted, adopting
adj. adoptive

☐ **advantage**
n. [ədvǽntidʒ]

adj. advantageous, advantaged

☐ **adventurous**
adj. [ədvéntʃərəs]

n. adventure, adventurer, venture
v. venture, ventured, venturing

☐ **adverse**
adj. [ədvɔ́ːrs]

n. adversity
adv. adversely

☐ **advise**	*n.* advice, adviser
v. [ədváiz]	*v.* advised, advising
	adj. advisory

| ☐ **affect** | *v.* affected, affecting |
| *v.* [əfékt] | |

| ☐ **affectionate** | *n.* affection |
| *adj.* [əfékʃənət] | *adv.* affectionately |

☐ **affirmative**	*n.* affirmation
n. adj. [əfɔ́ːrmətiv]	*v.* affirm, affirmed, affirming
	adv. affirmatively

| ☐ **affordable** | *v.* afford, afforded, affording |
| *adj.* [əfɔ́ːrdəbl] | |

| ☐ **aftermath** | = impact |
| *n.* [ǽftərmæθ] | |

| ☐ **afterward** | = afterwards |
| *adv.* [ǽftərwərd] | |

| ☐ **agreeable** | *v.* agree, agreed, agreeing |
| *adj.* [əgríːəbl] | *adv.* agreeably |

| ☐ **aimless** | *n.* aim |
| *adj.* [éimlis] | *v.* aim, aimed, aiming |

| ☐ **alcoholic** | *n.* alcohol, alcoholism |
| *n. adj.* [ælkəhɔ́ːlik] | |

| ☐ **alignment** | *v.* align, aligned, aligning |
| *n.* [əláinmənt] | |

| ☐ **allegedly** | *v.* allege, alleged, alleging |
| *adv.* [əlédʒidli] | *adj.* alleged |

| ☐ **allocation** | *v.* allocate, allocated, allocating |
| *n.* [æləkéiʃən] | |

☐ **allow**	*n.* allowance
v. [əláu]	*v.* allowed, allowing
	adj. allowable

| ☐ **allowance** | *v.* allow, allowed, allowing |
| *n.* [əláuəns] | |

| ☐ **along with** | = likewise |

| ☐ **alter** | *n.* alteration |
| *v.* [ɔ́ːltər] | *v.* altered, altering |

| ☐ **alternatively** | *n.* alternative, alternation |
| *adv.* [ɔːltɔ́ːrnətivli] | *v.* alternate, alternated, alternating |

| ☐ **altruism** | *n.* altruist |
| *n.* [ǽltruːìzm] | *adj.* altruistic |

| ☐ **amateur** | *n.* amateurism |
| *n. adj.* [ǽmətʃər] | *adj.* amateurish |

☐ **amazing**	*n.* amazement
adj. [əméiziŋ]	*v.* amaze, amazed, amazing
	adv. amazingly

| ☐ **ambiguous** | *n.* ambiguity |
| *adj.* [æmbígjuəs] | *adv.* ambiguously |

| ☐ **amend** | *n.* amendment |
| *v.* [əménd] | *v.* amended, amending |

| ☐ **amplifier** | *n.* amplification |
| *n.* [ǽmpləfàiər] | *v.* amplify, amplified, amplifying |

☐ **amusement**	*v.* amuse, amused, amusing
n. [əmjúːzmənt]	*adj.* amused, ammusing
	adv. amusingly

| ☐ **ancient** | *adv.* anciently |
| *n. adj.* [éinʃənt] | |

| ☐ **angular** | *n.* angle |
| *adj.* [ǽŋgjələr] | *adv.* angularly |

☐ **animated**	*n.* animation
adj. [ǽnəmèitid]	*v.* animate, animated, animating
	adv. animatedly

| ☐ **anniversary** | = jubilee |
| *n.* [æ̀nəvɔ́ːrsəri] | |

☐ **annual** *n. adj.* [ǽnjuəl]	*adv.* annually	☐ **article** *n.* [ɑ́ːrtikl]	= piece
☐ **antique** *n. adj.* [æntíːk]	*n.* antiquity	☐ **as such**	= accordingly
☐ **anxiously** *adv.* [ǽŋkʃəsli]	*n.* anxiety, anxiousness *adj.* anxious	☐ **as well**	= also
		☐ **assault** *n. v.* [əsɔ́ːlt]	*v.* assaulted, assaulting
☐ **apparently** *adv.* [əpǽrəntli]	*adj.* apparent	☐ **assertive** *adj.* [əsɔ́ːrtiv]	*n.* assertion *v.* assert, asserted, asserting *adv.* assertively
☐ **appeal** *n. v.* [əpíːl]	*v.* appealed, appealing *adj.* appealing		
☐ **appear** *v.* [əpíər]	*n.* appearance *v.* appeared, appearing *adj.* apparent	☐ **assignment** *n.* [əsáinmənt]	*v.* assign, assigned, assigning
☐ **apply for**	= call for	☐ **assistant** *n. adj.* [əsístənt]	*n.* assist, assistance *v.* assist, assisted, assisting
☐ **appreciate** *v.* [əpríːʃièit]	*n.* appreciation *v.* appreciated, appreciating *adj.* appreciable, appreciative *adv.* appreciably, appreciatively	☐ **assorted** *adj.* [əsɔ́ːrtid]	*n.* assortment *v.* assort, assorted, assorting
		☐ **at any rate**	= anyway
☐ **approachable** *adj.* [əpróutʃəbl]	*n.* approach *v.* approach, approached, approaching	☐ **attach** *v.* [ətǽtʃ]	*n.* attachment *v.* attached, attaching
		☐ **attend** *v.* [əténd]	*n.* attendance, attendant *v.* attended, attending *adj.* attendant
☐ **area** *n.* [ɛ́əriə]	= field		
☐ **argue** *v.* [ɑ́ːrgjuː]	*n.* argument *v.* argued, arguing *adj.* arguable *adv.* arguably	☐ **attendance** *n.* [əténdəns]	*n.* attendant *v.* attend, attended, attending *adj.* attendant
☐ **arise** *v.* [əráiz]	*v.* arise-arose-arisen, arising	☐ **attitude** *n.* [ǽtitjùːd]	*adj.* attitudinal
☐ **armed** *adj.* [ɑːrmd]	*n.* arm, arms, army *v.* arm, armed, arming *adj.* armless	☐ **attorney** *n.* [ətɔ́ːrni]	= advocate

□ **attractiveness** *n.* [ətrǽktivnis]	*n.* attraction *v.* attract, attracted, attracting *adj.* attractive *adv.* attractively	
□ **audience** *n.* [ɔ́ːdiəns]	*n.* audio	
□ **august** *adj.* [ɔːgʌ́st]	*adv.* augustly	
□ **author** *n. v.* [ɔ́ːθər]	*n.* authorship *v.* authored, authoring *adj.* authorial	
□ **authority** *n.* [əθɔ́ːrəti]	*n.* authorization *v.* authorize, authorized, authorizing *adj.* authoritarian, authoritative	
□ **autonomy** *n.* [ɔːtánəmi]	*adj.* autonomous *adv.* autonomously	
□ **available** *adj.* [əvéiləbl]	*n.* availability *v.* avail, availed, availing	
□ **average** *n. adj.* [ǽvəridʒ]	= mean	
□ **aviator** *n.* [éivièitər]	*n.* aviation *adj.* avian	
□ **avoid** *v.* [əvɔ́id]	*n.* avoidance *v.* avoided, avoiding *adj.* avoidable	
□ **award** *n. v.* [əwɔ́ːrd]	*n.* awardee *v.* awarded, awarding	
□ **awesome** *adj.* [ɔ́ːsəm]	*n.* awe *v.* awe, awed, awing *adv.* awesomely	
□ **bachelor** *n.* [bǽtʃələr]	= single	

□ **ballot** *n. v.* [bǽlət]	*v.* ballot, balloted, balloting
□ **ban** *n. v.* [bæn]	*v.* banned, banning
□ **barely** *adv.* [béərli]	*adj.* bare
□ **basis** *n.* [béisis]	*adj.* basic
□ **bay** *n.* [bei]	= cove
□ **beach** *n.* [biːtʃ]	*adj.* beachy
□ **bear** *v.* [bɛər]	*v.* bear-bore-born(e), bearing *adj.* bearable
□ **bear the brunt of**	= resist
□ **belong** *v.* [bilɔ́ːŋ]	*n.* belonging, belongings *v.* belonged, belonging
□ **bend** *v.* [bend]	*v.* bend, bent, bending
□ **beverage** *n.* [bévəridʒ]	= drink
□ **bias** *n.* [báiəs]	*adj.* biased
□ **bike** *n. v.* [baik]	*n.* biker *v.* biked, biking
□ **bitterly** *adv.* [bítərli]	*adj.* bitter
□ **bizarre** *adj.* [bizáːr]	*n.* bizarreness *adv.* bizarrely
□ **block** *n. v.* [blak]	*n.* blockade, blockage *v.* blocked, blocking

☐ **blonde**
n. adj. [bland]

= blond

☐ **blow**
n. v. [bloʊ]

v. blow-blew-blown, blowing

☐ **blown away**

= surprised

☐ **boost**
n. v. [buːst]

n. booster
v. boosted, boosting

☐ **bother**
v. [báðər]

v. bothered, bothering
adj. bothered, bothersome

☐ **boundary**
n. [báundri]

v. bound, bounded, bounding

☐ **bountiful**
adj. [báuntifəl]

n. bounty
adj. bounteous
adv. bountifully

☐ **brace**
n. v. [breis]

v. braced, bracing

☐ **bracket**
n. v. [brǽkit]

v. bracketed, bracketing

☐ **braid**
n. v. [breid]

v. braided, braiding

☐ **branch**
n. v. [brænʧ]

v. branched, branching

☐ **breeze**
n. [briːz]

= light wind

☐ **brewing**
n. [brúːiŋ]

n. brewery, brewer
v. brew, brewed, brewing

☐ **bribery**
n. [bráibəri]

v. bribe, bribed, bribing

☐ **brief**
n. v. adj. [briːf]

n. brevity
v. briefed, briefing
adv. briefly

☐ **bright**
adj. [brait]

n. brightness
v. brighten, brightened, brightening
adv. brightly

☐ **brilliant**
adj. [bríljənt]

n. brilliance
adv. brilliantly

☐ **broad**
adj. [brɔːd]

v. broaden, broadened, broadening
adv. broadly

☐ **brutal**
adj. [brúːtl]

n. brute, brutality
v. brutalize
adv. brutally

☐ **budget**
n. [bʌ́dʒit]

n. budgeting
adj. budgetary

☐ **bun**
n. [bʌn]

= round bread

☐ **burning**
n. adj. [bɔ́ːrniŋ]

n. burner
v. burn-burnt(burned)-burnt(burned), burning

☐ **business**
n. adj. [bíznis]

adj. busy

☐ **calamity**
n. [kəlǽməti]

adj. calamitous

☐ **calculate**
v. [kǽlkjulèit]

n. calculator, calculation
v. calculated, calculating
adj. calculable

☐ **campaign**
n. v. [kæmpéin]

n. campaigner
v. campaigned, campaigning

☐ **capacity**
n. adj. [kəpǽsəti]

adj. capacious

☐ **capital**
n. adj. [kǽpətl]

v. capitalize, capitalized, capitalizing

☐ **capricious**
adj. [kəpríʃəs]

n. caprice
adv. capriciously

☐ **capture** *n. v.* [kǽptʃər]	*n.* captor, captive, captivity, caption *v.* captured, capturing *adj.* captive	☐ **chat** *n. v.* [tʃæt]	*v.* chatted, chatting, chatter *adj.* chatty
☐ **career** *n.* [kəríər]	= job	☐ **cheery** *adj.* [tʃíəri]	*v.* cheer, cheered, cheering *adv.* cheerily
☐ **cargo** *n.* [káːrgou]	*n.* cargos(=cargoes)	☐ **chemical** *n. adj.* [kémikəl]	*n.* chemist, chemistry *adv.* chemically
☐ **carry** *n. v.* [kǽri]	*n.* carriage, carrier *v.* carried, carrying	☐ **chew** *n. v.* [tʃuː]	*v.* chewed, chewing *adj.* chewy, chewable
☐ **cautiously** *adv.* [kɔ́ːʃəsli]	*n.* caution, cautiousness *adj.* cautious	☐ **chilly** *adj.* [tʃíli]	*n.* chill, chilliness *v.* chill, chilled, chilling *adj.* chill
☐ **ceaseless** *adj.* [síːsləs]	*v.* cease, ceased, ceasing *adv.* ceaselessly	☐ **choreography** *n.* [kɔ̀(ː)riágrəfi]	*n.* choreographer *adj.* choreographic
☐ **celebrate** *v.* [séləbrèit]	*n.* celebration, celebrity *v.* celebrated, celebrating *adj.* celebratory, celebrated	☐ **cigarette** *n.* [sìgərét]	*n.* cigar
		☐ **circuit** *n. v.* [sə́ːrkit]	*v.* circuited, circuiting *adj.* circuitous, circuital
☐ **certain** *n. adj.* [sə́ːrtn]	*n.* certainty, certitude *v.* ascertain, ascertained, ascertaining *adv.* certainly	☐ **citizenship** *n.* [sítizənʃip]	*n.* citizen
		☐ **clear** *adj. v.* [kliər]	*n.* clearness, clearance, clarity *v.* cleared, clearing, clarify *adv.* clearly
☐ **chairman** *n. v.* [tʃéərmən]	*n.* chairmanship		
☐ **challenging** *adj.* [tʃǽlindʒiŋ]	*n.* challenge, challenger *v.* challenge, challenged, challenging	☐ **clichéd** *adj.* [kliːʃéid]	*n.* cliché
		☐ **clown** *n. v.* [klaun]	*v.* clowned, clowning *adj.* clownish
☐ **chaos** *n.* [kéias]	*adj.* chaotic *adv.* chaotically	☐ **coast** *n.* [koust]	*adj.* coastal
☐ **charm** *n. v.* [tʃaːrm]	*n.* charmer *v.* charmed, charming *adj.* charming *adv.* charmingly	☐ **cognitive** *adj.* [kágnitiv]	*n.* cognition *adv.* cognitively

☐ **coherent** adj. [kouhíərənt]	n. coherence adv. coherently		☐ **competent** adj. [kámpətənt]	n. competence, competency adv. competently
☐ **coincide** v. [kòuinsáid]	n. coincidence adj. coincident, coincidental adv. coincidentally		☐ **completely** adv. [kəmplíːtli]	n. completion, completeness v. complete, completed, completing adj. complete
☐ **colleague** n. [káliːg]	= co-worker		☐ **composed of**	= made up of
☐ **college** n. [kálidʒ]	adj. collegiate		☐ **comprehension** n. [kàmprihénʃən]	v. comprehend, comprehended, comprehending adj. comprehensible
☐ **combination** n. [kàmbənéiʃən]	v. combine, combined, combining			
☐ **comedian** n. [kəmíːdiən]	n. comedy, comic adj. comical, comedic		☐ **compressed** adj. [kəmprést]	n. compression, compressor v. compress, compressed, compressing adj. compressive
☐ **commitment** n. [kəmítmənt]	v. commit, committed, committing			
☐ **communism** n. [kámjunìzm]	n. communist		☐ **compulsory** adj. [kəmpálsəri]	n. compulsion v. compel, compelled, compelling adv. compulsorily
☐ **community** n. [kəmjúːnəti]	n. commune			
☐ **commute** n. v. [kəmjúːt]	n. commuter adj. commutable		☐ **concern** n. v. [kənsə́ːrn]	v. concerned, concerning adj. concerned prep. concerning
☐ **companion** n. [kəmpǽnjən]	n. companionship adj. companionable adv. companionably			
☐ **company** n. v. [kámpəni]	v. companied, companying		☐ **concrete** n. adj. v. [kánkriːt]	v. concreted, concreting adv. concretely
☐ **comparable** adj. [kámpərəbl]	n. comparability v. compare, compared, comparing adv. comparably		☐ **confuse** v. [kənfjúːz]	n. confusion v. confused, confusing
☐ **compassion** n. [kəmpǽʃən]	adj. compassionate adv. compassionately			

☐ **connect** *v.* [kənékt]	*n.* connection, connector, connectedness *v.* connected, connecting *adj.* connected	
☐ **consecutive** *adj.* [kənsékjutiv]	*adv.* consecutively	
☐ **consensus** *n.* [kənsénsəs]	*n.* consent *v.* consent, consented, consenting *adj.* consensual	
☐ **considerate** *adj.* [kənsídərət]	*n.* consideration *v.* consider, considered, considering *adv.* considerately	
☐ **consistently** *adv.* [kənsístəntli]	*n.* consistency *v.* consist, consisted, consisting *adj.* consistent	
☐ **constant** *n. adj.* [kánstənt]	*n.* constancy *adv.* constantly	
☐ **constituency** *n.* [kənstítʃuənsi]	*n.* constituent *adj.* constituent	
☐ **constitutional** *adj.* [kànstətú:ʃənl]	*n.* constitution *v.* constitute, constituted, constituting *adv.* constitutionally	
☐ **constraint** *n.* [kənstréint]	*v.* constrain, constrained, constraining	
☐ **consumption** *n.* [kənsʌ́mpʃən]	*n.* consumer *v.* consume, consumed, consuming	
☐ **contender** *n.* [kənténdər]	*v.* contend, contended, contending	

☐ **contentedly** *adv.* [kənténtidli]	*n.* contentment *v.* content, contented, contenting *adj.* contented	
☐ **continually** *adv.* [kəntínjuəli]	*n.* continuance, continuation, continuity *v.* continue, continued, continuing *adj.* continual, continuous	
☐ **contraceptive** *n. adj.* [kàntrəséptiv]	*n.* contraception	
☐ **contradictive** *adj.* [kàntrədíktiv]	*n.* contradiction *adv.* contradictively	
☐ **contradictory** *adj.* [kàntrədíktəri]	*v.* contradict, contradicted, contradicting	
☐ **contribute** *v.* [kəntríbjuːt]	*n.* contribution, contributor *v.* contributed, contributing *adj.* contributory	
☐ **controversial** *adj.* [kàntrəvə́ːrʃəl]	*n.* controversy *adv.* controversially	
☐ **conversation** *n.* [kànvərséiʃən]	*v.* converse, conversed, conversing *adj.* conversational	
☐ **coordinate** *n. adj.* [kouɔ́ːrdənət] *v.* [kouɔ́ːrdənèit]	*n.* coordination, coordinator *v.* coordinated, coordinating	
☐ **core** *n. v. adj.* [kɔr]	*v.* cored, coring *adj.* coreless	
☐ **corporation** *n.* [kɔ̀ːrpəréiʃən]	*adj.* corporate *v.* incorporate, incorporated, incorporating	

☐ **corrosive** *adj.* [kəróusiv]	*n.* corrosion, corrosiveness *v.* corrode, corroded, corroding *adv.* corrosively
☐ **cosmology** *n.* [kazmálədʒi]	*n.* cosmos, cosmologist *adj.* cosmological
☐ **costly** *adj.* [kɔ́ːstli]	*n.* cost *v.* cost-cost-cost, costing
☐ **courageous** *adj.* [kəréidʒəs]	*n.* courage *adv.* courageously
☐ **cover** *n. v.* [kʌ́vər]	*v.* covered, covering *adj.* coverable, covert, coverless
☐ **crafty** *adj.* [krǽfti]	*n.* craftiness *adv.* craftily
☐ **create** *v.* [kriéit]	*v.* created, creating *adj.* creative *adv.* creatively
☐ **creature** *n.* [kríːtʃər]	*n.* creator, creation, creativity
☐ **credibility** *n.* [krèdəbíləti]	*adj.* credible *adv.* credibly
☐ **crisis** *n.* [kráisis]	*adj.* critical *adv.* critically
☐ **critical** *adj.* [krítikəl]	*n.* critic *v.* criticize, criticized, criticizing *adv.* critically
☐ **criticism** *n.* [krítəsìzm]	*n.* critic *v.* criticize, criticized, criticizing *adj.* critical
☐ **cross over**	= traverse

☐ **crowded** *adj.* [kráudid]	*n.* crowd *v.* crowd, crowded, crowding
☐ **cruelty** *n.* [krúːəlti]	*adj.* cruel *adv.* cruelly
☐ **cryptography** *n.* [kriptágrəfi]	*n.* crypt *adj.* cryptic
☐ **cuisine** *n.* [kwizíːn]	= cooking
☐ **cultural** *adj.* [kʌ́ltʃərəl]	*n.* culture *adv.* culturally
☐ **curable** *adj.* [kjúərəbl]	*n.* cure *v.* cure, cured, curing *adj.* curative
☐ **curb** *n. v.* [kəːrb]	*v.* curbed, curbing
☐ **cure** *n. v.* [kjuər]	*v.* cured, curing *adj.* cured
☐ **curiosity** *n.* [kjùəriásəti]	*adj.* curious *adv.* curiously
☐ **current** *n. adj.* [kɔ́ːrənt]	*adv.* currently
☐ **curve** *n. v.* [kəːrv]	*v.* curved, curving *adj.* curvy
☐ **customer** *n.* [kʌ́stəmər]	= patron
☐ **damage** *n. v.* [dǽmidʒ]	*v.* damaged, damaging *adj.* damaging *adv.* damagingly
☐ **damned** *adj. adv.* [dæmd]	*n.* damnation *v.* damn, damned, damning
☐ **dazed** *adj.* [deizd]	*n.* daze *v.* daze, dazed, dazing

☐ **deal with**	= handle	
☐ **dearth** *n.* [dəːrθ]	= lack	
☐ **decline** *n. v.* [dikláin]	*v.* declined, declining	
☐ **decorative** *adj.* [dékərətiv]	*n.* decoration *v.* decorate, decorated, decorating *adv.* decoratively	
☐ **dedicated** *adj.* [dédikèitid]	*n.* dedication *v.* dedicate, dedicated, dedicating	
☐ **defensive** *adj.* [difénsiv]	*n.* defense, defensiveness *v.* defend, defended, defending *adv.* defensively	
☐ **define** *v.* [difáin]	*n.* definition *v.* defined, defining *adj.* definable	
☐ **delighted** *adj.* [diláitid]	*n.* delight *v.* delight, delighted, delighting *adj.* delightful *adv.* delightedly, delightfully	
☐ **deliver** *v.* [dilívər]	*n.* delivery, deliverer *v.* delivered, delivering *adj.* deliverable	
☐ **demonstration** *n.* [dèmənstréiʃən]	*n.* demonstrator *v.* demonstrate, demonstrated, demonstrating *adj.* demonstrable, demonstrative	
☐ **depend on**	= rely on	

☐ **depict** *v.* [dipíkt]	*n.* depiction *v.* depicted, depicting	
☐ **depressing** *adj.* [diprésiŋ]	*n.* depression *v.* depress, depressed, depressing *adj.* depressive *adv.* depressingly	
☐ **depth** *n.* [depθ]	*v.* deepen, deepened, deepening *adj.* deep *adv.* deeply	
☐ **descendant** *n.* [diséndənt]	*n.* descent *v.* descend, descended, descending	
☐ **describe** *v.* [diskráib]	*n.* description *v.* described, describing *adj.* descriptive, describable	
☐ **deserted** *adj.* [dizə́ːrtid]	*n.* desert, desertion *v.* desert, deserted, deserting	
☐ **destination** *n.* [dèstənéiʃən]	*n.* destiny *adj.* destined	
☐ **destroy** *v.* [distrɔ́i]	*n.* destruction, destroyer *v.* destroyed, destroying	
☐ **detail** *n. v.* [díːteil] *n. v.* [ditéil]	*v.* detailed, detailing *adj.* detailed	
☐ **deterioration** *n.* [ditìəriəréiʃən]	*v.* deteriorate, deteriorated, deteriorating	
☐ **determined** *adj.* [ditə́ːrmind]	*n.* determination *v.* determine, determined, determining	

develop v. [divéləp]	n. development, developer v. developed, developing
device n. [diváis]	v. devise, devised, devising
dialect n. [dáiəlèkt]	adj. dialectal
dice n. v. [dais]	v. diced, dicing
directly adv. [diréktli] adv. [dairéktli]	adj. direct v. direct, directed, directed
disability n. [dìsəbíləti]	v. disable, disabled, disabling adj. disabled
disadvantage n. [dìsədvǽntidʒ]	v. disadvantaged, disadvantaging adj. disadvantageous
disarray n. v. [dìsəréi]	= chaos
discharge n. v. [distʃá:rdʒ]	v. discharged, discharging
discomfort n. v. [diskΛmfərt]	v. discomforted, discomforting adj. uncomfortable
discount n. v. [dískaunt]	v. discounted, discounting adj. discountable
discovery n. [diskΛvəri]	v. discover, discovered, discovering adj. discoverable
discrimination n. [diskrìmənéiʃən]	v. discriminate, discriminated, discriminating
disease n. [dizí:z]	adj. diseased

disgustedly adv. [disgΛstidli]	n. disgust v. disgust, disgusted, disgusting adj. disgusting
disillusioned adj. [dìsilú:ʒənd]	n. disillusion, disillusionment v. disillusion, disillusioned, disillusioning
dismount v. [dismáunt]	v. dismount, dismounted, dismounting
disorder n. v. [disɔ́:rdər]	v. disordered, disordering adj. disorderly
dispose v. [dispóuz]	n. disposal, disposition, disposability v. disposed, disposing adj. disposable
disputable adj. [dispjú:təbl]	n. dispute, disputation v. dispute, disputed, disputing
disruptive adj. [disrΛptiv]	n. disruption, disruptiveness v. disrupt, disrupted, disrupting adj. disruptively
dissolve v. [dizálv]	n. dissolution v. dissolved, dissolving adj. dissolvable
distinction n. [distíŋkʃən]	n. distinctness adj. distinct, distinctive adv. distinctly, distinctively
distinguished adj. [distíŋgwiʃt]	v. distinguish, distinguished, distinguishing adj. distinguishable, distinguishing

☐ **district** *n.* [dístrikt]	= section
☐ **diversity** *n.* [divə́:rsəti] *n.* [daivə́:rsəti]	*adj.* diverse *adv.* diversely
☐ **divert** *v.* [divə́:rt] [daivə́:rt]	*n.* diversion, diverter *v.* diverted, diverting
☐ **dot** *n. v.* [dat]	*v.* dot, dotted, dotting *adj.* dotted
☐ **doubtful** *adj.* [dáutfəl]	*n.* doubt *v.* doubt, doubted, doubting *adv.* doubtfully
☐ **dramatic** *adj.* [drəmǽtik]	*n.* drama *adv.* dramatically
☐ **drawing** *n.* [drɔ́:iŋ]	*v.* draw-drew-drawn, drawing
☐ **drizzle** *n. v.* [drízl]	*v.* drizzled, drizzling *adj.* drizzly
☐ **drop** *n. v.* [drap]	*v.* dropped, dropping
☐ **drug** *n. v.* [drʌg]	*v.* drugged, drugging
☐ **easygoing** *adj.* [ì:zigóuiŋ]	= casual
☐ **eclipse** *n.* [iklíps]	*v.* eclipse, eclipsed, eclipsing
☐ **economist** *n.* [ikánəmist]	*n.* economy, economics *adj.* economic, economical *adv.* economically
☐ **elect** *v. adj.* [ilékt]	*n.* election, elector, electorate *v.* elected, electing *adj.* elective, electable, electoral *adv.* electorally

☐ **electrician** *n.* [ìlektríʃən]	*n.* electrics *v.* electrify, electrified, electrifying *adj.* electric *adv.* electrically
☐ **electron** *n.* [iléktra:n]	*n.* electronics *adj.* electronic, electronical *adv.* electronically
☐ **elementary** *adj.* [èləméntəri]	*n.* element *adj.* elemental
☐ **eliminate** *v.* [ilímənèit]	*n.* elimination *v.* eliminated, eliminating
☐ **elliptical** *adj.* [ilíptikəl]	*n.* ellipse, ellipsis *adv.* elliptically
☐ **eloquent** *adj.* [éləkwənt]	*n.* eloquence *adv.* eloquently
☐ **embarrass** *v.* [imbǽrəs]	*n.* embarrassment *v.* embarrassed, embarrassing *adj.* embarrassingly
☐ **embrace** *n. v.* [imbréis]	*v.* embraced, embracing
☐ **emotion** *n.* [imóuʃən]	*adj.* emotional, emotionless *adv.* emotionally
☐ **emphasize** *v.* [émfəsàiz]	*n.* emphasis *v.* emphasized, emphasizing *adj.* emphatic *adv.* emphatically
☐ **employee** *n.* [implɔ́ii:]	*n.* employer, employment *v.* employ, employed, employing *adj.* employable

☐ **empower** *v.* [impáuər]	*n.* empowerment *v.* empowered, empowering *adj.* empowering		☐ **ensure** *v.* [inʃúər]	*v.* ensured, ensuring
☐ **empty** *v. adj.* [émpti]	*n.* emptiness *v.* emptied, emptying *adv.* emptily		☐ **entertainer** *n.* [èntərtéinər]	*n.* entertainment *v.* entertain, entertained, entertaining
☐ **enable** *v.* [inéibl]	*n.* enablement, enabler *v.* enable, enabled, enabling *adj.* enabling		☐ **enthusiastic** *adj.* [inθù:ziǽstik]	*n.* enthusiasm, enthusiast *adv.* enthusiastically
☐ **encounter** *n. v.* [inkáuntər]	*v.* encountered, encountering		☐ **entire** *adj.* [intáiər]	*n.* entirety *adv.* entirely
☐ **encouraging** *adj.* [inkɔ́:ridʒiŋ]	*n.* encouragement *v.* encourage, encouraged, encouraging *adv.* encouragingly		☐ **entry** *n.* [éntri]	*v.* enter, entered, entering
			☐ **eradicate** *v.* [irǽdəkèit]	*n.* eradication *v.* eradicated, eradicating *adj.* eradicable
☐ **endorse** *v.* [indɔ́:rs]	*n.* endorsement *v.* endorsed, endorsing		☐ **error** *n.* [érər]	*v.* err, erred, erring *adj.* erroneous *adv.* erroneously
☐ **engage in**	= take part in		☐ **erstwhile** *adj. adv.* [ɔ́:rstwail]	= former
☐ **enhance** *v.* [inhǽns]	*n.* enhancement, enhancer *v.* enhanced, enhancing *adj.* enhanced		☐ **especially** *adv.* [ispéʃəli]	*adj.* especial, special
☐ **enlarge** *v.* [inlá:rdʒ]	*n.* enlargement *v.* enlarged, enlarging *adj.* enlarged		☐ **ethical** *adj.* [éθikəl]	*n.* ethics *adv.* ethically
			☐ **evaluate** *v.* [ivǽljuèit]	*n.* evaluation *v.* evaluated, evaluating
☐ **enlighten** *v.* [inláitn]	*n.* enlightenment *v.* enlightened, enlightening		☐ **even** *adj. adv.* [í:vən]	*adv.* evenly
☐ **enrich** *v.* [inrítʃ]	*n.* enrichment *v.* enriched, enriching		☐ **eventually** *adv.* [ivéntʃuəli]	*n.* event *adj.* eventual
☐ **enrollment** *n.* [inróulmənt]	*v.* enroll, enrolled, enrolling		☐ **evolution** *n.* [èvəlú:ʃən]	*v.* evolve, evolved, evolving *adj.* evolutionary *adv.* evolutionarily

☐ **exalt** *v.* [igzɔ́:lt]	*n.* exaltation *v.* exalted, exalting *adj.* exalted
☐ **exceptional** *adj.* [iksépʃənl]	*n.* exception *adv.* exceptionally
☐ **excessive** *adj.* [iksésiv]	*n.* excess *adj.* excess *adv.* excessively
☐ **exclusively** *adv.* [iksklú:sivli]	*n.* exclusion, exclusiveness *v.* exclude, excluded, excluding *adj.* exclusive
☐ **exempt** *v. adj.* [igzémpt]	*n.* exemption *v.* exempted, exempting
☐ **exercise** *n. v.* [éksərsàiz]	*v.* exercised, exercising
☐ **exhale** *v.* [ekshéil]	*n.* exhalation *v.* exhaled, exhaling
☐ **exhausted** *adj.* [igzɔ́:stid]	*n.* exhaustion *v.* exhaust, exhausted, exhausting *adj.* exhaustive *adv.* exhaustively
☐ **exit** *n. v.* [éksit] [égzɪt]	*v.* exited, exiting
☐ **expand** *v.* [ikspǽnd]	*n.* expansion, expanse *v.* expanded, expanding *adj.* expansive
☐ **experience** *n. v.* [ikspíəriəns]	*v.* experienced, experiencing *adj.* experienced, experiential
☐ **expire** *v.* [ikspáiər]	*n.* expiry *v.* expired, expiring
☐ **explanation** *n.* [èksplənéiʃən]	*v.* explain, explained, explaining *adj.* explanatory

☐ **explore** *v.* [iksplɔ́:r]	*n.* exploration *v.* explored, exploring *adj.* exploratory
☐ **exposure** *n.* [ikspóuʒər]	*v.* expose, exposed, exposing
☐ **express** *n. v. adj. adv.* [iksprés]	*n.* expression, expressionism *v.* expressed, expressing *adj.* expressive, expressible *adv.* expressly
☐ **extend** *v.* [iksténd]	*n.* extension, extent *v.* extended, extending *adj.* extensible, extensive *adv.* extensively
☐ **extinction** *n.* [ikstíŋkʃən]	*adj.* extinct
☐ **extract** *n.* [ékstrækt] *v.* [ikstrǽkt]	*n.* extraction *v.* extracted, extracting *adj.* extractive
☐ **extrovert** *n. adj.* [ékstrəvə̀:rt]	*n.* extroversion *adj.* extroverted
☐ **face** *n. v.* [feis]	*v.* faced, facing *adj.* facial *adv.* facially
☐ **facilitate** *v.* [fəsílətèit]	*n.* facility, facilitation, facilitator *v.* facilitated, facilitating
☐ **fairly** *adv.* [féərli]	*adj.* fair
☐ **familiarize** *v.* [fəmíljəràiz]	*n.* familiarization, familiarity *v.* familiarized, familiarizing *adj.* familiar *adv.* familiarly

☐ **fascinating** adj. [fǽsənèitiŋ]	n. fascination v. fascinate, fascinated, fascinating adv. fascinatingly	
☐ **fashionable** adj. [fǽʃənəbl]	n. fashion adv. fashionably	
☐ **faultless** adj. [fɔ́:ltləs]	n. fault adv. faultlessly	
☐ **faulty** adj. [fɔ́:lti]	n. fault adj. faultless	
☐ **feature** n. v. [fí:tʃər]	v. featured, featuring	
☐ **feckless** adj. [fékləs]	n. fecklessness adv. fecklessly	
☐ **firm** n. adj. [fə:rm]	n. firmness adv. firmly	
☐ **fitness** n. [fítnəs]	adj. fit	
☐ **fix** n. v. [fiks]	n. fixture, fixation v. fixed, fixing adj. fixable, fixed adv. fixedly	
☐ **flour** n. [fláuər]	adj. floury	
☐ **flourish** v. [flɔ́:riʃ]	v. flourished, flourishing	
☐ **flu** n. [flu]	n. influenza	
☐ **force** n. v. [fɔ:rs]	v. forced, forcing adj. forcible, forced adv. forcibly	
☐ **forgive** v. [fərgív]	n. forgiveness v. forgave, forgiving	
☐ **form** n. v. [fɔrm]	n. formation, format v. formed, forming adj. formal, formative	

☐ **formidable** adj. [fərmídəbl]	adv. formidably	
☐ **fort** n. [fɔ:rt]	n. fortress, fortification v. fortify, fortified, fortifying	
☐ **fortunate** adj. [fɔ́:rtʃənət]	n. fortune adv. fortunately	
☐ **found** v. [faund]	n. foundation, founder v. founded, founding adj. foundational	
☐ **fragrant** adj. [fréigrənt]	n. fragrance adv. fragrantly	
☐ **fraudulent** adj. [frɔ́:dʒulənt]	n. fraud, fraudulence adv. fraudulently	
☐ **frightened** adj. [fráitnd]	n. fright v. frighten, frightened, frightening adj. frightful	
☐ **frown** n. v. [fraun]	v. frowned, frowning	
☐ **fuel** n. v. [fjú:əl]	v. fueled, fueling	
☐ **full-time** adj. adv. [fùl táim]	n. full-timer	
☐ **fundamental** n. adj. [fʌ̀ndəméntl]	n. fundamentalism, fundamentalist adv. fundamentally	
☐ **gain** n. v. [gein]	v. gained, gaining adj. gainful	
☐ **garbage** n. [gá:rbidʒ]	= trash	
☐ **generally** adv. [dʒénərəli]	adj. general	
☐ **generous** adj. [dʒénərəs]	n. generosity adv. generously	

genetics	*n.* gene
n. [dʒənétiks]	*adj.* genetic
	adv. genetically

genre	= type
n. [ʒá:nrə]	

giant	*adj.* gigantic
n. adj. [dʒáiənt]	

giggle	*v.* giggled, giggling
n. v. [gígl]	*adj.* giggly

gleefully	*n.* glee
adv. [glí:fəli]	*adj.* gleeful

goal	= objective
n. [goʊl]	

government	*n.* governor, governance
n. [gʌ́vərnmənt]	*v.* govern, governed, governing
	adj. governing, governmental

grace	*v.* graced, gracing
n. v. [greis]	*adj.* gracious, graceful
	adv. graciously, gracefully

graffiti	*n.* graffito
n. [grəfí:ti]	

grasp	*v.* grasped, grasping
n. v. [græsp]	

grass	*v.* grassed, grassing
n. v. [græs]	

gratitude	*adj.* grateful
n. [grǽtətjù:d]	*adv.* gratefully

grin	*v.* grinned, grinning
n. v. [grin]	

grind	*n.* grinder
v. [graind]	*v.* ground, grinding

grocery	*n.* grocer
n. [gróusəri]	

grumpy	*adv.* grumpily
adj. [grʌ́mpi]	

guideline	= direction
n. [gáidlàin]	

hands-on	= firsthand
adj. [hǽndzən]	

handy	*n.* hand, handiness
adj. adv. [hǽndi]	*adv.* handily

happen	*n.* happening
v. [hǽpən]	*v.* happened, happening

harbinger	= omen
n. [há:rbindʒər]	

hardship	= adversity
n. [há:rdʃip]	

harm	*n.* harmfulness, harmlessness
n. v. [ha:rm]	*v.* harmed, harming
	adj. harmful, harmless
	adv. harmfully, harmlessly

harshly	*n.* harshness
adv. [há:rʃli]	*adj.* harsh

hay	*n.* haystack
n. [hei]	

helpless	*n.* help, helper
adj. [hélpləs]	*v.* help, helped, helping
	adj. helpful
	adv. helpfully, helplessly

heritage	*v.* inherit, inherited, inheriting
n. [héritidʒ]	*adj.* heritable

hide	*n.* hider
n. v. [haid]	*v.* hide-hid-hidden, hiding

hierarchy	*adj.* hierarchical
n. [háiərà:rki]	*adv.* hierarchically

☐ **historian** *n.* [histɔ́:riən]	*n.* history *adj.* historic, historical *adv.* historically
☐ **hold** *n. v.* [hould]	*v.* hold-held-held, holding
☐ **honorary** *adj.* [ánərèri]	*n.* honor *v.* honor, honored, honoring *adj.* honorable, honorific
☐ **hostile** *adj.* [hástl]	*n.* hostility *adv.* hostilely
☐ **however** *adv.* [hauévər]	= nevertheless
☐ **humble** *adj.* [hámbl]	*n.* humility *adv.* humbly
☐ **humid** *adj.* [hjú:mid]	*n.* humidity
☐ **humiliating** *adj.* [hju:mílièitiŋ]	*n.* humiliation *v.* humiliate, humiliated, humiliating
☐ **hydrogen** *n.* [háidrədʒən]	*v.* hydrate, hydrated, hydrating
☐ **hypocritical** *adj.* [hìpəkrítikəl]	*n.* hypocrite, hypocrisy *adv.* hypocritically
☐ **hypothesis** *n.* [haipáθəsis]	*v.* hypothesize, hypothesized, hypothesizing *adj.* hypothetical *adv.* hypothetically
☐ **ideology** *n.* [àidiálədʒi]	*adj.* ideological, ideologic *adv.* ideologically
☐ **ignition** *n.* [igníʃən]	*v.* ignite, ignited, igniting

☐ **ignorance** *n.* [ígnərəns]	*v.* ignore, ignored, ignoring *adj.* ignorant *adv.* ignorantly
☐ **illegal** *adj.* [ilí:gəl]	*adv.* illegally
☐ **illogical** *adj.* [iládʒikəl]	*adv.* illogically
☐ **illusion** *n.* [ilú:ʒən]	*adj.* illusionary, illusory
☐ **illustrate** *v.* [íləstrèit]	*n.* illustration, illustrator *v.* illustrated, illustrating *adj.* illustrative, illustrious
☐ **imitation** *n.* [ìmətéiʃən]	*n.* imitator *v.* imitate, imitated, imitating *adj.* imitative *adv.* imitatively
☐ **impairment** *n.* [impέərmənt]	*v.* impair, impaired, impairing *adj.* impaired
☐ **impatience** *n.* [impéiʃəns]	*adj.* impatient *adv.* impatiently
☐ **imperfect** *adj.* [impə́:rfikt]	*n.* imperfection *adj.* perfect *adv.* imperfectly
☐ **implication** *n.* [ìmplikéiʃən]	*v.* implicate, implicated, implicating
☐ **impress** *v.* [imprés]	*n.* impression *v.* impressed, impressing
☐ **impressive** *adj.* [imprésiv]	*n.* impression *v.* impress, impressed, impressing *adv.* impressively

improper *adj.* [imprápər]	*adv.* improperly	
improve *v.* [imprú:v]	*n.* improvement *v.* improved, improving	
impulse *n.* [ímpʌls]	*adj.* impulsive *adv.* impulsively	
in charge of	= responsible for	
in light of	= because of	
in particular	= especially	
in person	= personally	
include *v.* [inklú:d]	*n.* inclusion *v.* including *adj.* inclusive *adv.* inclusively	
inconceivable *adj.* [ìnkənsí:vəbl]	*adv.* inconceivably	
incredibly *adv.* [inkrédəbli]	*n.* incredibility *adj.* incredible	
incur *v.* [inkə́:r]	*n.* incurrence *v.* incurred, incurring	
independence *n.* [ìndipéndəns]	*adj.* independent *adv.* independently	
indicator *n.* [índikèitər]	*n.* indication *v.* indicate, indicated, indicating *adj.* indicative	
indifferent *adj.* [indífərənt]	*n.* indifference *adv.* indifferently	
individual *n. adj.* [ìndəvídʒuəl]	*n.* individualism *adv.* individually	
induce *v.* [indjú:s]	*n.* inducement *v.* induced, inducing	

industrialize *v.* [indʌ́striəlàiz]	*n.* industry, industrialization, industrialism *v.* industrialized, industrializing *adj.* industrial	
ineffective *adj.* [ìniféktiv]	*n.* ineffectiveness *adv.* ineffectively	
infamous *adj.* [ínfəməs]	*n.* infamy	
infant *n.* [ínfənt]	*n.* infancy *adj.* infantile	
infer *v.* [infə́:r]	*n.* inference *v.* inferred, inferring *adj.* inferable, inferential	
inferiority *n.* [infìərió:rəti]	*adj.* inferior	
influence *n. v.* [ínfluəns]	*n.* influencer *v.* influenced, influencing *adj.* influential	
inhabit *v.* [inhǽbit]	*n.* inhabitant, inhabitation *v.* inhabited, inhabiting *adj.* inhabitable, inhabited	
inherent *adj.* [inhíərənt]	*n.* inherence, inherency *v.* inhere, inhered, inhering *adv.* inherently	
injustice *n.* [indʒʌ́stis]	*n.* justice *adj.* unjust *adv.* unjustly	
inkling *n.* [íŋkliŋ]	= hunch	
insinuate *v.* [insínjuèit]	*n.* insinuation *v.* insinuated, insinuating	

☐ **inspiring**
adj. [inspáiəriŋ]

n. inspiration
v. inspire, inspired, inspiring
adj. inspired, inspirational

☐ **installation**
n. [ìnstəléiʃən]

n. installment
v. install, installed, installing

☐ **instance**
n. v. [ínstəns]

v. instanced, instancing

☐ **instead**
adv. [instéd]

= alternatively

☐ **instrument**
n. v. [ínstrəmənt]

n. instrumentation, instrumentalist
v. instrumented, instrumenting
adj. instrumental

☐ **integrate**
v. [íntəgrèit]

n. integration
v. integrated, integrating
adj. integrated

☐ **intellect**
n. [íntəlèkt]

n. intellectual
adj. intellectual
adv. intellectually

☐ **intend**
v. [inténd]

n. intention, intent
v. intended, intending
adj. intentional
adv. intentionally

☐ **interact**
v. [íntərækt]

n. interaction
v. interacted, interacting
adj. interactive
adv. interactively

☐ **interchange**
n. v. [ìntərtʃéindʒ]

n. interchangeability
v. interchanged, interchanging
adj. interchangeable
adv. interchangeably

☐ **interestingly**
adv. [íntərəstiŋli]

n. interest
v. interest, interested, interesting
adj. interesting

☐ **interference**
n. [ìntərfíərəns]

v. interfere, interfered, interfering

☐ **interlude**
n. [íntərlù:d]

= pause

☐ **intermediate**
n. adj. [ìntərmí:diət]

= middle

☐ **international**
adj. [ìntərnǽʃənəl]

adv. internationally

☐ **interrogation**
n. [ìntèrəgéiʃən]

n. interrogator
v. interrogate, interrogated, interrogating
adj. interrogatory, interrogative
adv. interrogatively

☐ **intolerance**
n. [intálərəns]

v. tolerate, tolerated, tolerating
adj. intolerant, intolerable
adv. intolerably

☐ **intoxicating**
adj. [intáksikèitiŋ]

n. intoxicant, intoxication
v. intoxicate, intoxicated, intoxicating

☐ **intrinsic**
adj. [intrínzik]

adv. intrinsically

☐ **introduction** n. [ìntrədʌ́kʃən]	v. introduce, introduced, introducing adj. introductory	☐ **irresponsible** adj. [ìrispánsəbl]	n. irresponsibility adv. irresponsibly
☐ **introvert** n. adj. [íntrəvə̀rt]	n. introversion adv. introverted	☐ **irreversible** adj. [ìrivə́ːrsəbl]	n. irreversibility adv. irreversibly
☐ **intrusion** n. [intrúːʒən]	n. intruder v. intrude, intruded, intruding adj. intrusive	☐ **irritate** v. [írətèit]	n. irritation v. irritated, irritating adj. irritated, irritating adv. irritatingly
☐ **intuition** n. [ìntjuːíʃən]	v. intuit, intuited, intuiting adj. intuitive adv. intuitively	☐ **isolation** n. [àisəléiʃən]	v. isolate, isolated, isolating adj. isolated
☐ **invasion** n. [invéiʒən]	n. invader v. invade, invaded, invading adj. invasive	☐ **item** n. [áitəm]	v. itemize, itemized, itemizing
☐ **invert** v. [invə́ːrt]	n. inversion, inverter v. inverted, inverting adj. inverse adv. inversely	☐ **justifiable** adj. [dʒʌ́stəfàiəbl]	n. justification v. justify, justified, justifying adv. justifiably
☐ **invisible** adj. [invízəbl]	n. invisibility adv. invisibly	☐ **juvenile** n. adj. [dʒúːvənl]	= adolescent
☐ **invoice** n. v. [ínvɔis]	v. invoiced, invoicing	☐ **latitude** n. [lǽtətjùːd]	adj. latitudinal adv. latitudinally
☐ **involve** v. [inválv]	n. involvement v. involved, involving	☐ **launch** n. v. [lɔːntʃ]	n. launcher v. launched, launching
☐ **irrational** adj. [irǽʃənl]	n. irrationality adv. irrationally	☐ **law** n. [lɔː]	n. lawyer adj. lawful adv. lawfully
☐ **irregular** adj. [irégjulər]	n. irregularity adv. irregularly	☐ **lead** n. v. adj. [liːd]	n. leader, leadership v. lead-led-led, leading
☐ **irrelevant** adj. [iréləvənt]	n. irrelevance adv. irrelevantly	☐ **league** n. [liːg]	= association
		☐ **lean** v. adj. [liːn]	v. leaned, leaning
		☐ **let** n. v. [let]	v. let-let-let, letting

librarian *n.* [laibréəriən]	*n.* library	

lift *n. v.* [lift]	*n.* lifter *v.* lifted, lifting *adj.* liftable

limit *n. v.* [límit]	*n.* limitation *v.* limited, limiting *adj.* limited, limiting, limitless

linger *v.* [líŋgər]	*v.* lingered, lingering *adj.* lingering *adv.* lingeringly

literacy *n.* [lítərəsi]	*n.* illiteracy *adj.* literate

literature *n.* [lítərətʃər]	*adj.* literary *adv.* literally

livestock *n.* [láivstak]	= farm animals

local *n. adj.* [lóukl]	*n.* locality, localization *v.* localize, localized, localizing *adv.* locally

located in	= situated in

logically *adv.* [ládʒikəli]	*n.* logic *adj.* logical

loyalist *n.* [lɔ́iəlist]	*n.* loyalty *adj.* loyal

made up of	= composed of

maintain *v.* [meintéin]	*n.* maintenance *v.* maintained, maintaining

majesty *n.* [mǽdʒəsti]	*adj.* majestic *adv.* majestically

malign *v. adj.* [məláin]	*v.* maligned, maligning *adj.* malignant

mammal *n.* [mǽməl]	*adj.* mammalian

manage to	= succeed in ~ing

mandatory *adj.* [mǽndətɔ̀:ri]	*v.* mandate, mandated, mandating

manufacturer *n.* [mænjufǽktʃərər]	*n.* manufacture *v.* manufacture, manufactured, manufacturing

many *n. adj.* [méni]	*adj.* many-more-most

march *n. v.* [ma:rtʃ]	*v.* marched, marching

massive *adj.* [mǽsiv]	*adv.* massively

match *n. v.* [mætʃ]	*v.* matched, matching *adj.* matchless

materialism *adj.* [mətíəriəlìzm]	*n.* material, materialist *adj.* materialist, materialistic

maximize *v.* [mǽksəmàiz]	*n.* maximum, maximization *v.* maximized, maximizing *adj.* maximal

means *n.* [mi:nz]	= method

mechanism *n.* [mékənìzm]	= system, device

medical *adj.* [médikəl]	*adv.* medically

medication *n.* [mèdəkéiʃən]	*n.* medicine *v.* medicate, medicated, medicating

medicinal *adj.* [mədísənl]	*n.* medicine

mediocrity *n.* [mì:diákrəti]	*adj.* mediocre	**moderately** *adv.* [mádərətli]	*n.* moderation *v.* moderate, moderated, moderating *adj.* moderate
melt *v.* [melt]	*v.* melted, melting	**modulation** *n.* [màdʒuléiʃən]	*v.* modulate, modulated, modulating
memorable *adj.* [mémərəbl]	*adv.* memorably	**molecule** *n.* [máləkjù:l]	*adj.* molecular
mention *n. v.* [ménʃən]	*v.* mentioned, mentioning *adj.* mentionable	**monetary** *adj.* [mánətèri]	*n.* money *adv.* monetarily
merciful *adj.* [mɔ́:rsifəl]	*n.* mercy, mercifulness	**monopoly** *n.* [mənápəli]	*n.* monopolization *v.* monopolize, monopolized, monopolizing
merciless *adj.* [mɔ́:rsiləs]	*n.* mercilessness *adv.* mercilessly	**morale** *n.* [mərǽl]	= confidence
merge *v.* [mə:rdʒ]	*n.* merger *v.* merged, merging	**mortality** *n.* [mɔːrtǽləti]	*n.* mortal *adj.* mortal *adv.* mortally
military *n. adj.* [mílitèri]	*adv.* militarily	**motion** *n. v.* [móuʃən]	*v.* motioned, motioning *adj.* motionless
mimic *v.* [mímik]	*n.* mimicry *v.* mimicked, mimicking	**motivate** *v.* [móutəvèit]	*n.* motivation, motivator *v.* motivated, motivating *adj.* motivational
mingle *v.* [míŋgl]	*v.* mingled, mingling	**movement** *n.* [mú:vmənt]	*v.* move, moved, moving
miniature *n. adj.* [míniətʃur]	*n.* miniaturization *v.* miniaturize, miniaturized, miniaturizing	**mud** *n.* [mʌd]	*v.* muddy, muddied, muddying *adj.* muddy
mishap *n.* [míshæp]	= accident	**municipal** *adj.* [mju:nísəpəl]	*n.* municipality *adv.* municipally
misunderstand *v.* [mìsʌndərstǽnd]	*n.* misunderstanding *v.* misunderstood, misunderstanding	**mustache** *n.* [mʌ́stæʃ]	*adj.* mustached
modeling *n.* [mádəliŋ]	*n.* model, modeler *v.* model, modeled, modeling		

☐ **mutation** *n.* [mju:téiʃən]	*v.* mutate, mutated, mutating *adj.* mutational	

☐ **mutation** *n.* [mju:téiʃən]	*v.* mutate, mutated, mutating *adj.* mutational
☐ **mutual** *adj.* [mjú:tʃuəl]	*n.* mutuality *adv.* mutually
☐ **mystery** *n.* [místəri]	*adj.* mysterious *adv.* mysteriously
☐ **mythical** *adj.* [míθikəl]	*n.* myth *adj.* mythological
☐ **nausea** *n.* [nɔ́:ziə]	*adj.* nauseous
☐ **nearsighted** *adj.* [níərsàitid]	*n.* nearsightedness
☐ **negligible** *adj.* [néglidʒəbl]	*n.* negligibility *v.* neglect, neglected, neglecting *adv.* negligibly
☐ **negotiate** *v.* [nigóuʃièit]	*n.* negotiation, negotiator *v.* negotiated, negotiating *adj.* negotiable
☐ **neighbor** *n. v. adj.* [néibər]	*n.* neighborhood *v.* neighbored, neighboring *adj.* neighborly
☐ **neurological** *adj.* [njùərəládʒikəl]	*n.* neurology, neurologist *adv.* neurologically
☐ **nonetheless** *adv.* [nʌnðəlés]	= nevertheless
☐ **normal** *n. adj.* [nɔ́:rməl]	*n.* normality, normalization *v.* normalize, normalized, normalizing *adv.* normally

☐ **notorious** *adj.* [noutɔ́:riəs]	*n.* notoriety *adv.* notoriously
☐ **nuisance** *n.* [nú:sns]	= annoyance
☐ **numerous** *adj.* [nú:mərəs]	*adv.* numerously
☐ **obesity** *n.* [oubí:səti]	*adj.* obese
☐ **obligation** *n.* [àbləgéiʃən]	*v.* oblige, obliged, obliging *adj.* obligational, obligatory
☐ **observant** *n. adj.* [əbzɔ́:rvənt]	*n.* observation, observance, observer, observatory *v.* observe, observed, observing *adj.* observational
☐ **obsession** *n.* [əbséʃən]	*v.* obsess, obsessed, obsessing *adj.* obsessive, obsessional *adv.* obsessively, obsessionally
☐ **obvious** *adj.* [ábviəs]	*n.* obviousness *adv.* obviously
☐ **occasionally** *adv.* [əkéiʒənəli]	*n.* occasion *adj.* occasional
☐ **occupy** *v.* [ákjupai]	*n.* occupancy, occupant, occupation *v.* occupied, occupying
☐ **occur** *v.* [əkɔ́:r]	*n.* occurrence *v.* occurred, occurring
☐ **offspring** *n.* [ɔ́fspriŋ]	= descendant

onset n. [á:nset]	= beginning	
optimism n. [áptəmìzm]	n. optimist adj. optimistic adv. optimistically	
option n. [ápʃən]	adj. optional adv. optionally	
orbital adj. [ɔ́:rbitl]	n. orbit adv. orbitally	
ordered adj. [ɔ́:rdərd]	n. order v. order, ordered, ordering adj. orderly	
orientation n. [ɔ̀:riəntéiʃən]	v. orient, oriented, orienting	
outbreak n. [áutbrèik]	= sudden happening	
outcome n. [áutkəm]	= consequence	
outset n. [áutset]	= beginning	
outspoken adj. [àutspóukən]	n. outspokenness adv. outspokenly	
outweigh v. [autwéi]	v. outweighed, outweighing	
overcast adj. [óuvərkæst]	= cloudy	
overflow n. [óuvərflòu] v. [òuvərflóu]	v. overflowed, overflowing adj. overflowing	
parade n. v. [pəréid]	v. paraded, parading	
parallel n. v. adj. adv. [pǽrəlèl]	v. paralleled, paralleling	

paralyze v. [pǽrəlàiz]	n. paralysis v. paralyzed, paralyzing adj. paralytic	
paramount adj. [pǽrəmàunt]	= outstanding	
participate v. [pɑːrtísəpèit]	n. participation, participant v. participated, participating adj. participatory	
partly adv. [pá:rtli]	n. part v. part, parted, parting	
part-time adj. adv. [pà:rt táim]	n. part-timer	
passage n. v. [pǽsidʒ]	v. pass, passed, passing	
passionate adj. [pǽʃənət]	n. passion adv. passionately	
patch n. v. [pætʃ]	v. patched, patching	
patiently adv. [péiʃəntli]	n. patience adj. patient	
pause n. v. [pɔ:z]	v. paused, pausing	
paw n. v. [pɔ:]	v. pawed, pawing	
pedestrian n. [pədéstriən]	= walker	
peek v. [pi:k]	v. peeked, peeking	
peninsula n. [pənínsələ]	adj. peninsular	
perceptive adj. [pərséptiv]	n. perception v. perceive, perceived, perceiving adv. perceptively	

☐ **perform** v. [pərfɔ́:rm]	n. performance, performer v. performed, performing
☐ **perpetually** adv. [pərpétʃuəli]	n. perpetuation v. perpetuate, perpetuated, perpetuating adj. perpetual
☐ **perseverance** n. [pə̀:rsəvíərəns]	v. persevere, persevered, persevering adj. persevering
☐ **persistence** n. [pərsístəns]	v. persist, persisted, persisting adj. persistent adv. persistently
☐ **personally** adv. [pɔ́:rsənəli]	v. personalize, personalized, personalizing adj. personal
☐ **personnel** n. [pə̀:rsənél]	= staff
☐ **perspective** n. adj. [pərspéktiv]	adv. perspectively
☐ **persuasion** n. [pərswéiʒən]	v. persuade, persuaded, persuading adj. persuasive adv. persuasively
☐ **pharmacy** n. [fá:rməsi]	n. pharmacist, pharmaceutical adj. pharmaceutical
☐ **phase** n. v. [feiz]	v. phased, phasing
☐ **physical** adj. [fízikəl]	n. physics, physicist, physician adv. physically

☐ **physiological** adj. [fìziəládʒikəl]	n. physiology adv. physiologically
☐ **pinpoint** n. v. adj. [pínpɔint]	v. pinpointed, pinpointing
☐ **pitch** n. v. [pitʃ]	n. pitcher v. pitched, pitching
☐ **planet** n. [plǽnit]	adj. planetary
☐ **platform** n. [plǽtfɔːrm]	= podium
☐ **plausible** adj. [plɔ́:zəbl]	n. plausibility adv. plausibly
☐ **plot** n. v. [plat]	n. plotter v. plotted, plotting
☐ **podium** n. [póudiəm]	= platform
☐ **pool** n. v. [puːl]	v. pooled, pooling
☐ **position** n. v. [pəzíʃən]	v. positioned, positioning adj. positional
☐ **possible** adj. [pásəbl]	n. possibility adv. possibly
☐ **practitioner** n. [præktíʃənər]	= expert
☐ **precaution** n. [prikɔ́:ʃən]	adj. precautionary
☐ **precedent** n. adj. [présədənt]	v. precede, preceded, preceding
☐ **precious** adj. [préʃəs]	= valuable
☐ **precisely** adv. [prisáisli]	n. precision, preciseness adj. precise

□ **predictive**	= anticipating	
adj. [pridíktiv]		

□ **preferably**	*n.* preference
adv. [préfərəbli]	*v.* prefer, preferred, preferring
	adj. preferable

□ **prejudice**	= bias
n. [prédʒudis]	

□ **prelude**	= prologue
n. [préljuːd]	

□ **present**	*v.* presented, presenting
n. adj. [préznt]	
v. [prizént]	*adv.* presently

□ **presentation**	*n.* presenter
n. [prèzəntéiʃən]	*v.* present, presented, presenting
	adj. presentational

□ **preservation**	*n.* preservative
n. [prèzərvéiʃən]	*v.* preserve, preserved, preserving

□ **prevalent**	*n.* prevalence
adj. [prévələnt]	*v.* prevail, prevailed, prevailing
	adv. prevalently

□ **preventable**	*n.* prevention
adj. [privéntəbl]	*v.* prevent, prevented, preventing
	adj. preventive

□ **previously**	*adj.* previous
adv. [príːviəsli]	

□ **primarily**	*n.* primary
adv. [praimérəli]	*adj.* primary

□ **priority**	*v.* prioritize, prioritized, prioritizing
n. [praió:rəti]	*adj.* prior

□ **prisoner**	*n.* prison
n. [prízənər]	

□ **privilege**	*v.* privileged, privileging
n. v. [prívəlidʒ]	*adj.* privileged

□ **procedure**	*v.* proceed, proceeded, proceeding
n. [prəsíːdʒər]	*adj.* procedural

□ **process**	*n.* processor
n. v. [práses]	*v.* processed, processing

□ **product**	*n.* produce, producer, production
n. [prádʌkt]	*v.* produce, produced, producing
	adj. productive
	adv. productively

□ **progressive**	*n.* progressiveness, progression
adj. [prəgrésiv]	*v.* progress, progressed, progressing
	adv. progressively

□ **prominent**	*n.* prominence
adj. [prámənənt]	*adv.* prominently

□ **promising**	*v.* promise, promised, promising
adj. [prámisiŋ]	*adv.* promisingly

□ **pronunciation**	*v.* pronounce, pronounced, pronouncing
n. [prənʌnsiéiʃən]	

□ **prop**	*v.* propped, propping
n. v. [prap]	

□ **propagate**	*n.* propaganda, propagation
v. [prápəgèit]	*v.* propagated, propagating

□ **provide**	*n.* provider
v. [prəváid]	*v.* provided, providing

□ **proximity**	*adj.* proximate
n. [praksíməti]	

☐ **pyramid** *n.* [pírəmìd]	*adj.* pyramidal	

| ☐ **qualification**
 n. [kwàləfikéiʃən] | *v.* qualify, qualified, <br> qualifying |

| ☐ **radically**
 adv. [rǽdikli] | *adj.* radical |

| ☐ **radius**
 n. [réidiəs] | *adj.* radial
 adv. radially |

| ☐ **raised**
 adj. [reizd] | *v.* raise, raised, raising |

| ☐ **rally**
 n. v. [rǽli] | *v.* rallied, rallying |

| ☐ **rank**
 n. v. [ræŋk] | *v.* ranked, ranking |

| ☐ **readily**
 adv. [rédəli] | *n.* readiness
 adj. ready |

| ☐ **realism**
 n. [rí:əlìzm] | *n.* realist, reality
 adj. real, realistic
 adv. realistically |

| ☐ **reasonable**
 adj. [rí:zənəbl] | *n.* reason, reasoning
 v. reason, reasoned, <br> reasoning
 adv. reasonably |

| ☐ **recall**
 n. v. [rí:kɔːl] | *v.* recalled, recalling |

| ☐ **receive**
 v. [risíːv] | *n.* receipt, reception
 v. received, receiving
 adj. receptive |

| ☐ **recommendation**
 n. [rèkəmendéiʃən] | *v.* recommend, <br> recommended, <br> recommending
 adj. recommended |

| ☐ **recreational**
 adj. [rèkriéiʃənl] | *n.* recreation |

| ☐ **reduce**
 v. [ridúːs] | *n.* reduction
 v. reduced, reducing
 adj. reducible |

| ☐ **refuse**
 v. [rifjúːz] | *n.* refusal
 v. refused, refusing |

| ☐ **regarding**
 prep. [rigáːrdiŋ] | = concerning |

| ☐ **related to** | = connected to |

| ☐ **relative**
 n. adj. [rélətiv] | *n.* relativity
 v. relate, related, <br> relating
 adj. relatively |

| ☐ **religion**
 n. [rilídʒən] | *adj.* religious
 adv. religiously |

| ☐ **reluctant**
 adj. [rilʌ́ktənt] | *n.* reluctance
 adv. reluctantly |

| ☐ **reminiscent**
 adj. [rèmənísnt] | *n.* reminiscence
 v. reminisce, <br> reminisced, <br> reminiscing |

| ☐ **remorse**
 n. [rimɔ́ːrs] | *adj.* remorseful, <br> remorseless
 adv. remorsefully, <br> remorselessly |

| ☐ **renewable**
 adj. [rinúːəbl] | *n.* renewal
 v. renew, renewed, <br> renewing |

| ☐ **renowned**
 adj. [rináund] | *n.* renown |

| ☐ **repeat**
 n. v. [ripíːt] | *n.* repetition
 v. repeated, repeating
 adj. repetitive
 adv. repeatedly |

| ☐ **replaceable**
 adj. [ripléisəbl] | *n.* replacement
 v. replace, replaced, <br> replacing |

☐ **replicate** v. [répləkèit]	n. replicator, replication v. replicated, replicating adj. replicable	
☐ **reputation** n. [rèpjutéiʃən]	n. repute adj. reputational, reputed, reputable	
☐ **requirement** n. [rikwáiərmənt]	v. require, required, requiring adj. requisite	
☐ **residency** n. [rézədənsi]	n. resident, residence v. reside, resided, residing adj. residential	
☐ **resident** n. [rézədnt]	n. residency, residence v. reside, resided, residing adj. residential	
☐ **resilience** n. [rizíljəns]	adj. resilient adv. resiliently	
☐ **resourceful** adj. [risɔ́:rsfəl]	n. resourcefulness v. resource, resourced, resourcing adv. resourcefully	
☐ **respect** n. v. [rispékt]	v. respected, respecting adj. respectful, respectable adv. respectfully, respectably	
☐ **response** n. [rispáns]	n. respondent, respondence v. respond, responded, responding adj. responsive	
☐ **restless** adj. [réstləs]	n. rest, restlessness v. rest, rested, resting adv. restlessly	

☐ **restriction** n. [ristríkʃən]	v. restrict, restricted, restricting adj. restrictive adv. restrictively	
☐ **restructure** n. v. [rì:strʌ́ktʃər]	n. restructuring v. restructured, restructuring	
☐ **result in**	= bring about	
☐ **retain** v. [ritéin]	n. retention v. retained, retaining	
☐ **retrace** v. [ritréis]	v. retraced, retracing adj. retraceable	
☐ **retrieve** v. [ritrí:v]	n. retrieval, retriever v. retrieved, retrieving adj. retrievable	
☐ **revise** v. [riváiz]	n. revision v. revised, revising	
☐ **revival** n. [riváivəl]	v. revive, revived, reviving	
☐ **rewarding** adj. [riwɔ́:rdiŋ]	n. reward v. reward, rewarded, rewarding adv. rewardingly	
☐ **rhyme** n. v. [raim]	v. rhymed, rhyming adj. rhymeless	
☐ **rightly** adv. [ráitli]	n. v. adj. adv. right	
☐ **ripe** v. adj. [raip]	n. ripeness v. ripen, ripened, ripening	
☐ **rosy** adj. [róuzi]	n. rosiness adv. rosily	
☐ **rotary** n. adj. [róutəri]	v. rotate, rotated, rotating	
☐ **rotten** adj. [rátn]	n. rot v. rot, rotted, rotting	

☐ **roughly** *adv.* [rʌ́fli]	*adj.* rough	
☐ **royal** *n. adj.* [rɔ́iəl]	*n.* royalty *adv.* royally	
☐ **rumor** *n. v.* [rúːmər]	*v.* rumored, rumoring	
☐ **runway** *n.* [rʌ́nwèi]	= track	
☐ **sacred** *adj.* [séikrid]	*n.* sacredness	
☐ **scan** *n. v.* [skæn]	*n.* scanner *v.* scanned, scanning	
☐ **scarcity** *n.* [skéərsəti]	*adj.* scarce *adv.* scarcely	
☐ **scenery** *n.* [síːnəri]	*n.* scene	
☐ **scent** *n. v.* [sent]	*v.* scented, scenting *adj.* scentless	
☐ **scholarship** *n.* [skálərʃip]	*n.* scholar *adj.* scholarly	
☐ **screen** *n. v.* [skriːn]	*n.* screening *v.* screened, screening	
☐ **scruffy** *adj.* [skrʌ́fi]	*n.* scruff, scruffiness *adv.* scruffily	
☐ **secretary** *n.* [sékrətèri]	*adj.* secretarial	
☐ **sector** *n. v.* [séktər]	*v.* sectored, sectoring *adj.* sectoral	
☐ **sedentary** *adj.* [sédntèri]	= inactive	
☐ **seed** *n. v.* [siːd]	*n.* seedling *v.* seeded, seeding *adj.* seedless	

☐ **sensation** *n.* [senséiʃən]	*n.* sense *v.* sense, sensed, sensing *adj.* sensational *adv.* sensationally	
☐ **sentence** *n. v.* [séntəns]	*v.* sentenced, sentencing *adj.* sentential, sententious	
☐ **serene** *adj.* [səríːn]	*n.* serenity *adv.* serenely	
☐ **service** *n. v. adj.* [sə́ːrvis]	*v.* serviced, servicing	
☐ **settler** *n.* [sétlər]	*v.* settle, settled, settling	
☐ **shell** *n. v.* [ʃel]	*v.* shelled, shelling	
☐ **shift** *n. v.* [ʃift]	*v.* shifted, shifting *adj.* shifty	
☐ **shine** *v.* [ʃain]	*v.* shine-shone(shined)-shone(shined), shining *adj.* shiny	
☐ **shovel** *n. v.* [ʃʌ́vəl]	*v.* shoveled, shoveling	
☐ **shower** *n. v.* [ʃáuər]	*v.* showered, showering *adj.* showery	
☐ **significantly** *adv.* [signífikəntli]	*n.* significance *adj.* significant	
☐ **simulate** *v.* [símjuleit]	*n.* simulation, simulator *v.* simulated, simulating	
☐ **simultaneously** *adv.* [sàiməltéiniəsli]	*adj.* simultaneous	
☐ **situation** *n.* [sìtʃuéiʃən]	*v.* situate, situated, situating *adj.* situational	

□ **skeptical** *adj.* [sképtikəl]	*n.* skeptic, skepticism *adv.* skeptically	
□ **skill** *n.* [skil]	*adj.* skilled, skillful *adv.* skillfully	
□ **skip** *n. v.* [skip]	*v.* skipped, skipping	
□ **slam** *v.* [slæm]	*v.* slammed, slamming	
□ **sober** *v. adj.* [sóubər]	*n.* sobriety, soberness *v.* sobered, sobering *adv.* soberly	
□ **solid** *n. adj.* [sálid]	*n.* solidarity, solidity, solidness *v.* solidify, solidified, solidifying	
□ **solution** *n.* [səlúːʃən]	*v.* solve, solved, solving *adj.* soluble	
□ **sophisticated** *adj.* [səfístəkèitid]	*n.* sophistication *adv.* sophisticatedly	
□ **specialized** *adj.* [spéʃəlàizd]	*n.* specialization *v.* specialize, specialized, specializing *adj.* special	
□ **specific** *adj.* [spəsífik]	*n.* specification *v.* specify, specified, specifying *adv.* specifically	
□ **spectacular** *adj.* [spektǽkjulər]	*n.* spectacle *adv.* spectacularly	
□ **spectator** *n.* [spékteitər]	*v.* spectate, spectated, spectating	
□ **spending** *n.* [spéndiŋ]	*v.* spend, spended, spending	
□ **spike** *n. v.* [spaik]	*v.* spiked, spiking *adj.* spiked, spiky	

□ **splendid** *adj.* [spléndid]	*adv.* splendidly
□ **sporting** *adj.* [spɔ́ːrtiŋ]	*n.* sports *v.* sport, sported, sporting
□ **spouse** *n.* [spaus]	*adj.* spousal
□ **spray** *n. v.* [sprei]	*n.* sprayer *v.* sprayed, spraying
□ **squander** *n. v.* [skwándər]	*v.* squandered, squandering
□ **squeaky** *adj.* [skwíːki]	*v.* squeak, squeaked, squeaking
□ **stability** *n.* [stəbíləti]	*n.* stabilization *v.* stabilize, stabilized, stabilizing *adj.* stable
□ **standard** *n. adj.* [stǽndərd]	*n.* standardization *v.* standardize, standardized, standardizing
□ **standing** *n. adj.* [stǽndiŋ]	*v.* stand-stood-stood, standing
□ **stare** *v.* [stɛər]	*v.* stared, staring
□ **state** *n. v. adj.* [steit]	*n.* statement, statehood *v.* stated, stating *adj.* stately
□ **status** *n.* [stéitəs]	*n.* state
□ **steel** *n. v. adj.* [stiːl]	*v.* steeled, steeling
□ **stereotype** *n. v.* [stériətàip]	*v.* stereotyped, stereotyping
□ **stern** *adj.* [stəːrn]	*n.* sternness *adv.* sternly

☐ **stipend** *n.* [stáipend]	= salary	☐ **sufficiently** *adv.* [səfíʃəntli]	*n.* sufficiency *adj.* sufficient
☐ **stretch** *n. v.* [stretʃ]	*n.* stretcher *v.* stretched, stretching	☐ **suggestion** *n.* [səgdʒéstʃən]	*v.* suggest, suggested, suggesting *adj.* suggestive
☐ **strive** *v.* [straiv]	*n.* strife *v.* strive- strove(strived)- striven(strived), striving	☐ **suitable** *adj.* [sú:təbl]	*n.* suitability *v.* suit, suited, suiting *adv.* suitably
☐ **stroll** *n. v.* [stroul]	*n.* stroller *v.* strolled, strolling	☐ **superior** *n. adj.* [supíəriər]	*n.* superiority
☐ **struggle** *n. v.* [strʌgl]	*v.* struggled, struggling	☐ **supervision** *n.* [sù:pərvíʒən]	*n.* supervisor *v.* supervise, supervised, supervising *adj.* supervisory
☐ **stubbornness** *n.* [stʌ́bərnnəs]	*adj.* stubborn *adv.* stubbornly		
☐ **stuff** *n. v.* [stʌf]	*n.* stuffiness, stuffing *v.* stuffed, stuffing *adj.* stuffy, stuffed	☐ **supply** *n. v.* [səplái]	*n.* supplier *v.* supplied, supplying
☐ **stunning** *adj.* [stʌ́niŋ]	*v.* stun, stunned, stunning *adj.* stunned *adv.* stunningly	☐ **support** *n. v.* [səpó:rt]	*n.* supporter *v.* supported, supporting *adj.* supportive
☐ **subordinate** *n. adj.* [səbó:rdənət] *v.* [səbó:rdənèit]	*n.* subordination, subordinator *v.* subordinated, subordinating	☐ **supportive** *adj.* [səpó:rtiv]	*n.* supportiveness *adv.* supportively
		☐ **surely** *adv.* [ʃúərli]	*adj.* sure
☐ **subsequently** *adv.* [sʌ́bsikwəntli]	*adj.* subsequent	☐ **surgery** *n.* [sɔ́:rdʒəri]	*n.* surgeon *adj.* surgical *adv.* surgically
☐ **suburban** *adj.* [səbə́:rbən]	*n.* suburb		
☐ **sudden** *adj.* [sʌdn]	*n.* suddenness *adv.* suddenly	☐ **surplus** *n. adj.* [sɔ́:rplʌs]	= extra
		☐ **survival** *n. adj.* [sərváivəl]	*n.* survivor *v.* survive, survived, surviving
☐ **suffering** *n.* [sʌ́fəriŋ]	*n.* sufferer *v.* suffer, suffered, suffering	☐ **suspension** *n.* [səspénʃən]	*v.* suspend, suspended, suspending

sustenance *n.* [sʌ́stənəns]	*n.* sustainability *v.* sustain, sustained, sustaining *adj.* sustainable
swiftly *adv.* [swíftli]	*n.* swiftness *adj.* swift
swine *n.* [swain]	= pig
symbol *n.* [símbəl]	*n.* symbolism *v.* symbolize, symbolized, symbolizing *adj.* symbolic
symptom *n.* [símptəm]	*v.* symptomize, symptomized, symptomizing *adj.* symptomless, symptomatic
synonymous *adj.* [sinánəməs]	*n.* synonym, synonymy *adv.* synonymously
talent *n.* [tǽlənt]	*adj.* talented
task *n. v.* [tæsk]	*v.* tasked, tasking
temperate *adj.* [témpərət]	*n.* temperance *adv.* temperately
temperature *n.* [témpərətʃər]	*adj.* temperate
tenable *adj.* [ténəbl]	= defensible
territory *n.* [térətɔːri]	*adj.* territorial
terror *n.* [térər]	*n.* terrorism, terrorist *v.* terrify, terrified, terrifying *adj.* terrible, terrific

tertiary *adj.* [tɔ́ːrʃieri]	= third
theory *n.* [θíːəri]	*n.* theorist *v.* theorize, theorized, theorizing *adj.* theoretical *adv.* theoretically
therapy *n.* [θérəpi]	*n.* therapist *adj.* therapeutic *adv.* therapeutically
though *adv. conj.* [ðou]	*conj.* although
thoughtless *adj.* [θɔ́ːtləs]	*n.* thoughtlessness *adv.* thoughtlessly
throat *n.* [θrout]	*adj.* throaty *adv.* throatily
tiresome *adj.* [táiərsəm]	*v.* tire, tired, tiring *adv.* tiresomely
totality *n.* [toutǽləti]	*n.* total *adj.* total *adv.* totally
touched *adj.* [tʌtʃt]	*v.* touch, touched, touching
toughness *n.* [tʌ́fnəs]	*v.* toughen, toughened, toughening *adj.* tough *adv.* toughly
trade *n. v. adj.* [treid]	*n.* trader, tradesman, trading *v.* traded, trading
trail *n. v.* [treil]	*n.* trailer *v.* trailed, trailing

transition *n.* [trænzíʃən]	*n.* transit *v.* transit, transited, transiting, transition, transitioned, transitioning *adj.* transitional, transitory
transitive *adj.* [trǽnsətiv]	*n.* transitivity *adv.* transitively
trap *n. v.* [træp]	*v.* trapped, trapping
travel *n. v.* [trǽvəl]	*n.* traveler *v.* traveled, traveling
treatment *n.* [trí:tmənt]	*n.* treat *v.* treat, treated, treating *adj.* treatable
tremendously *adv.* [triméndəsli]	*adj.* tremendous
trend *n.* [trend]	*adj.* trendy, trending
tribe *n.* [traib]	*adj.* tribal *adv.* tribally
trustworthy *adj.* [trʌ́stwɜ̀rði]	*n.* trustworthiness
tunnel *n. v.* [tʌ́nl]	*v.* tunneled, tunneling
tutor *n. v.* [tjú:tər]	*n.* tutoring, tutorial *v.* tutored, tutoring
twist *n. v.* [twist]	*v.* twisted, twisting *adj.* twisty
typically *adj.* [típikəli]	*n.* type *adj.* typical
unanswerable *adj.* [ʌnǽnsərəbəl]	*adj.* answerable
undeniable *adj.* [ʌndináiəbəl]	*adv.* undeniably

undermine *v.* [ʌ̀ndərmáin]	*v.* undermined, undermining
undertake *v.* [ʌ́ndərtèik]	*n.* undertaking, undertaker *v.* undertake-undertook -underfaken, undertaking
undue *adj.* [ʌndú]	*n.* due *adj.* due
unfortunately *adv.* [ʌnfɔ́rtʃənətli]	*adj.* unfortunate
union *n.* [jú:njən]	*v.* unionize, unionized, unionizing
unlikely *adj.* [ʌnláikli]	*n.* unlikeliness, unlikelihood
unnecessarily *adv.* [ʌnnésəsèrəli]	*adj.* unnecessary, necessary
unproductive *adj.* [ʌnprədʌ́ktiv]	*adj.* productive *adv.* unproductively
unreasonably *adv.* [ʌnrízənəbli]	*n.* unreasonableness *adj.* unreasonable, reasonable
unscrupulous *adj.* [ʌ̀nskrupjóləs]	*n.* unscrupulousness *adv.* unscrupulously
unsustainable *adj.* [ʌ̀nsəstéinəbl]	*adv.* unsustainably
unwise *adj.* [ʌ̀nwáiz]	*adj.* unwisely
uphold *v.* [ʌ̀phóuld]	*n.* upholder *v.* uphold-upheld- upheld, upholding
upward *adj. adv.* [ʌ́pwərd]	*adv.* upwardly
usually *adv.* [jú:ʒuəli]	*adj.* usual